BOBBY'S TRIALS

BOBBY WILSON, JD

Publisher: Apache Publishing Company

www.apachepublishingcompany.com

ISBN: 1-4392-6118-0
ISBN-13: 9781439261187
Library of Congress Control Number: 2009910575

BOBBY'S TRIALS

BOBBY WILSON, JD

The incredible story of a poor teenage Oklahoma farm boy who was charged with murdering his mother and sister in cold blood and then burning down the family home in a supposed attempt to cover up his crimes—and his ten-year court battle to clear his name.

"An absolutely spellbinding true-life drama"
Amazon.com

This is a true story, the actual names of the participants are used.

The locations are as described, and incidents discussed herein really occurred.

If anyone described feels slandered or libeled that is too bad.

The laws concerning this area of law are very clear:

"The truth is an absolute defense to defamation claims".

The Author

CONTENTS

DEDICATION

To my beloved wife, for her commitment to me and her tenacity in bringing this book to completion.

I dedicate this book to the handful of noble gentlemen mentioned herein who stepped forward on my behalf during this ordeal to help a poor and naive teenage boy, who was caught up in a maelstrom that nearly overwhelmed him.

I also express my gratitude to the brave and open-minded jurors who served during my trials and closely followed the evidence introduced at those trials and disregarded the mostly false and misleading newspaper accounts of these events in their local media.

And to Earl Warren, the fourteenth chief justice of the United States Supreme Court, who, even though he was a district attorney and attorney general for almost twenty years himself, knew from experience that Constitutional Safeguards needed to be established to protect the young and innocent from the widespread law enforcement abuse taking place in the United States during the sixties. This story is an excellent example of such abuse.

INTRODUCTION

I reached the age of sixty-five this year and suddenly realized that if I did not tell my story, no one ever would. And what a story it is. Someone once said truth is stranger than fiction, and that certainly applies to my story.

I had planned to take the witness stand in court in 1973, during what would have been my third and final trial. I would have told for the first time what really happened to my family and me in those early morning hours of June 19, 1963. Fate intervened, and I was never given the opportunity to tell my story in court. I am not sure if that was a blessing or a curse.

If you have ever wondered what life was like in 1963 in a small town in Oklahoma for an indigent teenager accused of murdering his own mother and sister, just read this book. And then, afterward, thank your lucky stars you were never in my shoes.

CHAPTER 1
Confusion

• • •

THE HELLHOLE OF A JAIL smelled of urine and rotting mattresses as usual. Tonight, there was an additional scent in the air. It was the smell of fear and impending violence. I was familiar with that odor, having sensed it often in this place. Caged men give off the same odor as frightened livestock in a corral when they smell a slaughterhouse.

I knew earlier in the day that as soon as dark arrived and the downstairs jailer and his wife had gone to bed that it would not be a peaceful night, at least not for me. My evening plans were made earlier that day when the deputies opened the cellblock doors into the main bullpen and they ushered Jimmy and Johnny, the twins, into the large bullpen main cell. The twins had glanced over at me seated in my usual window perch in the far corner of the bullpen. They had quickly looked away, showing no signs of recognition, never making eye contact with me. But I knew and they knew we had unfinished business. It had been years since our last violent encounter, and now I was easy prey, with no one to come to my rescue. What was it the Indian said in that old Western movie? "Today is a good day to die." Somehow, that thought did not seem very comforting. Eighteen is too young an age to die.

I correctly surmised what Jimmy and Johnny would spend the remainder of their day doing. They would recruit some helpers from this septic tank of human refuse since two-to-one odds were not good enough for them. Then they would come after me. No school-ground teacher would save me this time, and I would not be fighting to protect my sister's chastity. This time, I would be fighting for my life. There would be no quarter given, none asked.

It was not a long wait. I could hear the twins moving from cell to cell, making conversation with each prisoner, sizing them up as an ally or a rat. By the end of the day, the twins had found the thief and his two cellmates. Their conversations became muted and confidential, not a good sign. "Birds of a feather" seemed an accurate description of the group of plotters.

I had caught the thief the night before stealing out of the paper sack of personal items under my cell bunk. I had grabbed his hair with my left hand and pulled his head from under my bunk and hissed, "You are a dead man." Then I slammed my right fist into his chest, knocking him backward, out of my cell. He scrambled back to his feet, dropping or throwing my two candy bars on the floor. He had avoided me all day, unsure if I was finished with him.

I had not seen Jimmy or Johnny in several years. I heard they had been expelled from junior high school. That had not surprised me. My last face-to-face meeting with the twins was the last day my sister and I attended the country school. I had refused to return to that school for fear of what they might do to my sister.

Reality suddenly appeared in front of me in the form of the twins and their new allies.

"Let's hang the bastard!" Jimmy shouted.

"Yeah," joined in his twin brother.

"We will make it look like a suicide; everyone will think the sorry-ass hung himself."

"Bobby, we are going to do you a favor and put you out of your misery," the thief chimed in, careful to stay out of my reach.

The three of them started moving toward me. I stood up from my perch and backed into the corner of the bullpen so no one could get behind me.

Johnny removed his leather belt and fashioned a noose and began looking for an adequate ceiling water pipe support. Two more of their buddies joined in behind them. *Another quiet evening at home,* I thought to myself. As strange as it sounds, you can get accustomed to almost anything, even fighting for your life on a daily basis. I guess combat soldiers understand that feeling.

My whole being became focused on the twins' hands and feet. If I had learned anything while rotting away in jail, it was never take your eyes off your attacker's hands and feet. To do so would mean you could not react fast enough to the attack, and the first person to land a solid fist or boot to a vital part of another's body was probably going to prevail. You never see the second or third blows coming, and by then you are on the ground, to be kicked into submission or death, whichever comes first. A torn kidney is not a pleasant way to bleed to death.

I had not said a word yet—after all, what was there to say? The twins knew I would put up a fight. The only question was, how much of a fight? They had not forgotten the country school episode years earlier, and neither had I. It was unfinished business, left to fester all these years.

I knew Jimmy would make the first move to attack. Johnny would follow his lead. The three other thugs fanned out to the sides of the twins. All of them slowly moved toward me as I waited for Jimmy to make his move. I was going to try to block his move and jam my right thumb and trigger finger in both his eyes and then squeeze those digits together until he passed out, hopefully blinding him and putting him out of the fight; a little trick I had learned and used from necessity. Then I would body-blow Johnny and turn my attention to the three punks with a screaming attack, not unlike that of a crazed man fighting for his life.

And then the strangest thing happened. James, the black kid, stuck his hand through the cell bars behind me and slid an unopened knife into my right hand. I pressed the button, and the unmistakable sound of a switchblade knife opening stopped all movement in the bullpen. I brought the six-inch blade level with Jimmy's stomach. I moved toward Jimmy with the knife in a menacing manner. He and Johnny turned and quickly departed to their cells, almost stumbling over their other retreating comrades.

It was over as quickly as it started. I walked over to James and slipped his now closed knife through the bars. I whispered, "Thanks," and he grinned and nodded. I never knew where he got the knife or how he got it into the jail, and I never asked. Being a jail trustee had its benefits. I guess the fact I never called him nigger and had been the only white guy willing to play checkers with him and share my cell's bunk bed had paid off for me, big time. He would save my bacon again, one day in the future, by simply mailing a letter for me.

I suddenly felt weak, and my legs started to tremble, so I went into my cell and lay down on my bunk, with one eye on the cell door in case someone else decided to invade my space that night. I had survived another day. I wondered what tomorrow would bring. One sure thing, it wouldn't be anything pleasant. My life had become a daily struggle to survive.

The noise and squeals from the other end of the cellblock indicated the twins and their three friends had turned their attention and animal urges toward the young gay kid, who had been trying to remain as quiet and unseen as possible. His criminal offense of public intoxication that day was being punished by a gang rape by the five animals while the jailer and wife slept peacefully below. I attended the same middle school as Johnnie, the kid; we were the same age. I had wondered about his feminine ways. Now my suspicions were confirmed, and he was learning that the meek are not going to inherit the earth.

I stared at the bottom of James' empty overhead bunk and wondered how I came to be in such a mess. Why me? What had I ever done to deserve this? Why was I so alone? I had never felt more confused in all my eighteen years.

Sure, I had been confused before, like when I was five years old and my father walked out, never to return. That was confusing, until Mother explained, "All men are bastards."

Or the time shortly after my eighth birthday, when we were on the run from my supposed stepfather, and Mother handed me a rifle, a real one, and told me to stand guard and shoot any man who bothered her. That was confusing until Mother explained that my supposed stepfather, like all men, was a bastard.

Or the times Mother invited strange men to our home and told Sister and me to entertain the ones she did not take to her bedroom. That was confusing until Mother explained, "All men are bastards, but sometimes you have to use them."

Or the time when Mother took her butcher knife and cut the throat of my show bull. That was confusing, until she explained, "You're a bastard just like your father."

But my current state of confusion was by far the worst I ever encountered. My brain was just not working; I would shake my head and pinch myself constantly. I must have looked and acted deranged. Maybe I was. I was in a fog, a very thick fog.

Why was everyone constantly asking me, "Bobby, what happened?"

I really just wanted it to be over, to wake up and find myself alone in my old steel-rail single bed. I would look out my bedroom window and see the sunrise and the sparkle of the dew on the fields. Butch would be on the back porch watching me through my bedroom window, patiently waiting for me to bring him something to eat, or better still, take him hunting.

I tried to focus my mind and memory on the events in my life that led to my current state of turmoil. How did a kid born in San Francisco, California, in 1944 end up in Oklahoma in Indian Country in 1963? And how did he, at the ripe old age of eighteen, end up charged with murdering his mother and sister, his only known family, and not have a memory of those tragic events? Something very complicated had occurred in my mind, and I needed to unravel this mystery. Then maybe I could explain to the world what had happened on that fateful morning. I forced my mind to retrace the past events of my life that led to the current disaster.

———

CHAPTER 2

Beginnings

• • •

MY FATHER WALKED OUT ON the day of my fifth birthday. No party, no gifts, just the image in my mind of him arguing with Mother and walking out the front door of our small frame home in Sacramento, California. He just walked away with no suitcase, no good-byes, no nothing. He had not actually lived there as far as I can remember.

I ran to the front window and pressed my face to the windowpane and watched him walk down our driveway; he stopped and turned to look at me. Our eyes locked for an instant. He turned away and walked out of sight in the drizzling rain. That was my first and last image of him. It is burned into my memory. No photos of him existed or ever appeared, since Mother had none.

He was stocky, about 180 pounds, five feet ten, a clean-cut man and well dressed in a gray raincoat. His hair was dark with a receding front hairline; he wore his hair short and kept it combed neat. Mother sat at the kitchen table, staring at nothing, hands shaking and anger in her face. I walked up to her.

"Where is Father going?" I asked.

"To hell," was her immediate bitter reply. I was not sure then where that place was, but I would learn one day.

Mother jumped up and started packing our clothes into our three suitcases, one large leather monogrammed monster for her, and two smaller suitcases for Sister and me. It did not take long. We did not own much. We loaded into a taxicab, which took us to the local Greyhound bus station, and within an hour, the bus drove away with us through the wet drizzle that is Sacramento, California, in September.

The bus drove north into the dark green forests of Northern California, into Oregon State, ending our trip in Eugene, Oregon. For reasons unknown, it was now our new home. The only conversation coming from Mother on our road trip to Oregon was a constant reference to the sorry bastard, our father, who had abandoned us for the last time.

Mother found new housing, but I do not remember the details. I only remember her working as a waitress in a local hotel restaurant. She found new men to entertain, but no one in particular. Men came and men went over the next several years.

I started the first grade in school on my sixth birthday. I was born on Labor Day. Most of the other first graders had already had some home schooling or had gone to kindergarten, and I was immediately aware that I was the only boy in the class who could not write or spell his own name.

One of Mother's boyfriends had given me a cheap leather belt on which he branded my name on the rear portion. Each time I needed to write my name on a class assignment I had to remove I had to remove my belt and look on the back to see how to spell my name, which was pretty complicated—Bobby— at least it was to me. I had no clue how to spell my last name.

Sister was terrified at the thought of going to school the following year, but I spent time with her, teaching her to write her name and what I had learned about reading, writing, and numbers, so she would not be as embarrassed as I had been.

Sister and I had no home instruction or schooling because Mother said she dropped out of school in her third year to work in the fields, so she was not much help on anything to do with reading, writing, and numbers.

When Sister enrolled in the first grade the next fall, she was very frightened. I stayed with her as much as I could on the school grounds to reassure her that she would be fine. Most of the other first and second grade children were from middle-class families, and everyone seemed to get along and enjoyed games and the playground activities. At least now, Sister and I looked forward to going to school each day, not so much for learning but for the social contact with other children, playtimes and recesses. We began to feel more settled.

One day, Mother introduced a new man to Sister and me. Bill was more than just another date. Mother said he was our new dad!

Bill was in the U.S. Air Force, a career man with sergeant stripes, I was told. Mother announced, "All four of us are driving to Vermont to live on an air force base." It sounded like a place we would love, with snow and lakes and a wonderful new life.

Bill did not look at all like our *last dad*; he was tall, skinny, balding, and somewhat ugly. He was older than Mother. He was a quiet man who had very little to say to Sister and me. He had never had a family before, so this was a *new experience* for him. But he did own a new 1949 two-door Ford Coupe.

A week later, all four of us loaded up that Ford Coupe and hit the road. My only remembrance of driving to Vermont was that it must have been on the far side of the world. The drive became an endurance contest, day after day of mindless driving. The Ford seemed to get smaller each day. It had no radio. Mother and Bill alternated driving and sat in the front seat, talking all day. Sister and I sat in the back seat, watching everything go by. We discovered we could not play cards or word puzzles while driving because it made us car sick. We could only sit, watch, and be bored. We would stop several times a day to eat sandwiches and go to the bathroom.

Once we finally reached Vermont, we settled into a small, furnished air force house near Ethan Allen Air Force

Base. Mother did not have to work anymore. Life became more settled and routine, except for Mother's temper and my occasional beatings, usually with coat hangers. I never got used to them; they hurt. Mother had a hair-trigger temper whenever I did something to upset her. In fact, she had a hair-trigger temper whenever anyone upset her. I usually just tried to avoid being around her unless I had no choice.

The woods around our home were full of chipmunks, and I soon had many four-legged friends. Sister would watch in amazement as my furry friends soon learned to eat food out of my hands or crawl into my pocket and help themselves.

Bill and I occasionally threw softballs back and forth to each other. He usually worked all night and slept during the day, so I never really spent much time getting to know him.

He took Sister and me fishing at a nearby lake, a lake so big I could not see across to the other side. We caught fish, but they had fish worms so we could not eat them.

Bill gave me the first birthday present I ever received. He bought me a fishing pole with hooks, sinkers, and a little tackle box on my eighth birthday. He also bought Sister a doll and doll stuff for her seventh birthday.

Airplanes fascinated me, and I begged Bill to take me to the air force base so I could watch the planes take off and land. He finally gave in and was able to convince the gate guard that his "son" needed to see the base doctor. I spent the day watching him and his crew work on air force fighter planes. Those old prop-driven birds were left over from World War II but were used during the Korean War.

Bill explained to me that the old fighters were being converted into interceptors, and after he and his crews were finished working on them, they would be used to intercept Russian bombers who might try to penetrate the East Coast of the United States. Bill tried to explain to me that he had fought the Commies in Korea during the Korean War and that the little devils wanted to take over the entire world. I told him I was sure the interceptors would make short work of those awful Commies, whoever they were.

When it was time to quit for the day, he and his crew headed for the showers to clean up. I tagged along and was shocked to see grown men walking around naked in the showers. I had never seen men naked before, and seeing all that black hair and those *man things*, I felt a little inadequate. I had seen Mother naked many times. She paraded around the house without a stitch on, like it was the normal thing to do. But these naked men, that was pretty shocking to me. Bill noticed me gawking at the men, and he took me to the men's mess hall next door and told me to wait there. He told me it might be better not to mention to Mother what I saw in the showers that day, so I kept it secret.

I guess the quiet life did not sit well with Mother. Late one night, she suddenly awoke Sister and me from the bed we shared. Bill was on duty at the base.

"The military police are here," Mother announced. "They are here to question you about the *bad things* Bill has been doing to the both of you." Mother told us she would tell the military police what Bill had done, and we only had to shake our heads in agreement, unless of course, we wanted our "butts busted."

Mother brought the two uniformed military policemen into our bedroom, where Sister and I stood shivering in our pajamas, more from fright than from the cool night air. The two policemen wrote as Mother talked. We nodded our heads when they asked us to verify what Mother told them about Bill touching our private places. They finished writing, and Mother signed their reports. After they left, I asked Mother what Bill had done and why the policemen were asking so many questions. She told me, "Shut up. Start packing your suitcases. We're getting the hell out of town."

By daylight, we had everything we could load in Bill's Ford, and we drove away, fast. Mother told me to watch the cars behind us and see if any of them were following us. I did not see anything suspicious but kept watch anyway.

Mother stopped a few miles out of town to a gas up the Ford, and when she walked into the station, I asked Sister if Bill had done anything to her. She said she didn't remember anything. I didn't, either. Bill never hit or touched me. Mother always did enough hitting for both of them. Mother never mentioned what had *really happened* between the two of them. I was afraid to ask, so was Sister. Bill was the only dad Sister and I would ever encounter. We never saw or heard from him again. I missed him. He probably missed his Ford Coupe, too.

Mother drove like a woman possessed, with one eye always on the rear-view mirror. We crossed the state line, and it was suddenly daylight. We stopped at the first hardware store that was open. Mother left us in the Ford and grabbed her purse and said, "Stay put, and keep your eyes open and the doors locked."

She returned carrying a long narrow box and a small sack. She handed the box and sack to me in the back seat. "Open the box, read the instructions, and load the damn thing," she told me. We quickly resumed our road trip.

I opened the long box at one end and discovered to my astonishment the butt end of a rifle. "It's a gun!" I shouted. I was excited, confused, and a little scared. I pulled the Winchester .22 single-shot bolt-action rifle out of its box. Its barrel was not very long, just my size.

Mother seemed frantic as we drove through the countryside, and she barked instructions to me in the back seat.

"Bobby, read those damn instructions and learn how to load and use it. We may need it soon. There are boxes of bullets in the sack. Bill is probably following us. He will kill me if he catches us."

I had never seen or even handled a real gun before, but with boyhood enthusiasm, I proceeded to examine the rifle and its instruction manual.

Mother looked at me sternly in the rear-view mirror. "You are now the man of the house, and Sister and I are depending on you to protect us." Mother's voice had an urgent sound to it, and in an instant, I knew my childhood was over. I was now *the man of the house*, whether I was ready or not. I studied the rifle's manual and the little rifle closely. Luckily, the manual was mostly in pictures, since my reading ability was very limited. I could barely read comic books. I had missed many days of school, and so had Sister. We had not attended any school in months.

We traveled west, stopping only for food, gas, or bathroom breaks, sleeping in the Ford Coupe whenever possible, sometimes parked alongside the road. After two days on the road, Mother seemed to relax somewhat, and we began to stop every few hours. Those stops gave me a chance to learn how to aim and shoot my rifle. After a few hours of practice, shooting tin cans and such, I had mastered the little rifle. Mother was impressed with my skill, and I taught her how to shoot it. She instructed me to always keep it loaded and ready: "We may need it." I pointed out to her that such behavior was against the safe handling procedures outlined in the manual, but her reply was, "What use is an empty gun? Always keep it loaded." I always did. That rule would one day save my life.

Sister was afraid of guns, and of most things in life for that matter, so she was not interested in learning how to shoot the little rifle, even though I offered to teach her. Sister was painfully shy and somewhat frail in stature. She would talk to me whenever we were alone; otherwise, she avoided all contact with people. She loved animals. She was very afraid of Mother, not that Mother ever beat her, because I never remembered that happening. Mother did not have to spank Sister in order to intimidate her. Sister saw the beatings I received. All Mother had to do was look at Sister and raise her voice. That was more than sufficient. Sister never talked back to Mother, but I did occasionally and paid the price. I never talked disrespectfully to Mother. I would simply point out to her that sometimes her actions did not make any sense, at least to me. Mother would then grab the handiest weapon, such as a belt or clothes hanger and proceed to beat the "holy hell," as she called it, out of me. Often I could not sit down for hours due to the pain and welts on my backside. Sister would turn away during those episodes, but she got the message.

Sister would never talk to a stranger. If she and I went into a store or to a neighbor's home, I always had to speak for her, because she would just sit or stand there and shake her head when people asked her a question or tried to talk to her. I never knew her to have any friends or playmates; she just entertained herself and visited her own little world. Sister grew and developed into a teenager, but she never lost her shyness around people or her fear of Mother. I worried about how she would manage on her own if Mother or I were not around. She was the picture of innocence.

I suspected Mother hated all men, and I was just a smaller version of *those bastards*. I seemed to be a constant irritant to her. She stared at me at times, and if I questioned her, she would say, "You are just like your father—look like him and act like him." Those statements made me feel uneasy and a little frightened. I was not proud to be my father's son; after all, he was our enemy and had abandoned us.

Mother instructed me to always keep the loaded rifle under my bed wherever we stayed and to always be ready to use it if Bill or some man ever bothered me. "Can I count on you?" she would continually ask me. I hoped I could stand tall and be able to protect her when the time came.

The journey was pretty boring to Sister and me, just a never-ending asphalt strip of Highway 66. It might have helped to have someone along to explain the passing countryside to us. Mother knew nothing of the countryside, nor did she care to discuss it. We never stopped to explore new places.

The Ford developed a leaking tail pipe, and the engine exhaust fumes began making all of us car sick. An easy solution would have been to stop and have it repaired. But Mother was not to be delayed. Several times, Sister and I passed out, probably from breathing the fumes. Sister needed to stop by the roadside and vomit every hour or so. Her carsickness stops probably saved all of us from carbon monoxide poisoning.

One evening, we turned into a roadside motel for the night. Mother had been particularly edgy that day. After we unloaded our suitcases, Mother announced she would need to be *out* for several hours, and Sister and I were to get in our bed and go to sleep. When it was dark outside, she then drove away to parts unknown.

It did not take Sister and me long to fall asleep since it was such a treat to sleep in a real bed after several days of sleeping in the back seat of the Ford. There was no TV or radio in the cheap motel room, so there was nothing to do but sleep.

Something woke me in the middle of the night. I heard voices or noises or something. It was light enough in the motel room to see; the outside neon lights caused an eerie glow in the room, a mixture of red and white pulsating light. I looked over at the other bed, and it was empty, the covers having never been disturbed. Mother was not there. I felt so alone and a little scared.

I eased out of bed, trying not to wake Sister, and I looked out the front window. I saw the outline of our Ford parked in front of our door. There was enough light to reveal movement in the front seat, and the vehicle was rocking, much like a mechanic rocks a car when testing the shocks.

Remembering Mother's standing orders to me, I was immediately concerned that she was in danger and ran and grabbed my loaded rifle from under my bed. I was trembling as I opened the front door, careful to prop a suitcase in the doorway so I would not lock myself out of the motel room. I could hear the voices of a man and woman coming from the car. There was a frantic sound to the voices, and the Ford Coupe was really rocking now. I crept up to the passenger window and raised my head up just high enough to peer inside and see a man on top of Mother. Her legs were around his back, and she was obviously fighting for her life. I tried to open the car door, but it was locked. I began to panic. I was supposed to protect Mother. I cocked the hammer on the rifle and pulled the trigger. Luckily, the barrel was pointing up and no one was shot. The sharp crack of the gunshot immediately brought results. The rocking stopped, the frantic voices stopped, and all was quiet. Lights began to come on in the other motel rooms, and their window curtains parted; faces appeared.

The passenger-side window of our car suddenly rolled down, and Mother hissed, "Bobby, what the hell are you doing?" Her voice had a sharp edge to it.

"Protecting you," was my quivering response. I opened the rifle bolt, and the empty shell flew into the air as I fumbled to reload the .22. I remembered Mother's words, "What use is an empty gun?"

"Bobby, it is all right. I am okay. Go back into the room and put the gun up. I will be there in a minute." Her voice had lost its edge, but she seemed impatient with me.

I turned and walked back into the room and shut the door. Sister was sitting up in bed, looking frightened. I explained to her that I had to save Mother from a strange man, but everything was okay now and she could go back to sleep.

I was now wide-awake. I lay in bed waiting for Mother for an hour or so before falling asleep; she was still outside. She was in her bed when I awoke at first light.

Protecting Mother and Sister was stressful on me, although I was not sure what the danger was. She must have allowed that man to get in the Ford with her since she never tried to get away from him. That puzzled me.

The motel manager came early that morning and asked us to *please leave*. Mother argued with him about the posted check-out time and then slammed the door in his face. We loaded up and hit the road. Mother never mentioned the incident, nor did I.

The Ford crawled west on Highway 66 until it and we were exhausted. We were back where we started, Eugene, Oregon, land of loggers and constant wetness.

In less than one year, we had driven from the far West Coast to the far East Coast and back again. Not an easy task in a two-door Ford Coupe with everything we owned stuffed into three suitcases.

It was refreshing to see the evergreen forests and the logging trucks as we neared home.

We drove around the university town until dark before Mother located a small two-bedroom apartment. The apartment was on the lower floor of a three-story older frame home that had been converted into apartments, no doubt because of its proximity to the campus of the University of Oregon, located a few blocks away.

Our landlord was a friendly man named Sherman. He even helped me carry in our suitcases, all three of them.

Sherman was an old bachelor, about forty-five years old, with a balding head. He had converted his family's home into apartments after his parents passed away. He had lived there all his life. He was now living in the upstairs apartment.

He took care of all maintenance, yard work, and upkeep on the old house with its large, fenced-in, grassy backyard.

In a few days, it became apparent that Sherman had something in common with Sister and me: loneliness. He did not have any visitors or friends, and soon Sherman and I became friends and business partners.

Mother had immediately gone to work as a waitress in a local hotel restaurant/lounge in Eugene. Sister was content to put together boxes of puzzles that Sherman had supplied us.

I was now nine years old. I had been broke all my life, and I was ready to make some spending money since Mother never had any to share, and I always felt uneasy asking her for any. I confided in Sherman that we were broke and I needed to earn some money since I was now the *man of the house*. I asked Sherman if he needed to hire my services. "Well," Sherman replied, "I don't, but I have an idea, if you don't mind getting your hands dirty."

"Not a problem," I replied, never having any fear of playing in the dirt. "When do I start?"

Sherman proceeded to counsel me on the little-known art of fishing-worm gathering. "The local fishermen love to use live large worms to catch fish. The king of all fishing worms are called night crawlers, but they only come out of the ground at night, and only after rain. You gotta be quick if you want to catch one. They'll come wriggling out of their holes part way, and if you aren't fast they'll pop back underground before you can get a hold on them. Sometimes they'll get a death grip on their holes. You must be fast, but gentle, or else you will pull the worm into pieces, and then it has no value. If the worm has a death grip on his hole, you must rub the worm's exposed belly, and he will release his ground grip and surrender."

"So how do we make money catching worms?" I asked. I was a little uneasy; this might have been a big joke, especially the belly-rubbing part.

"Sell them at the local fishing stores. The stores pay fifty cents per dozen for those juicy crawlers. The stores box 'em and sell 'em." Sherman half-grinned and asked, "When do you want to get started?"

"Right now! Show me where to find the worms," I replied excitedly.

"Not so fast. You can only collect night crawlers at night, and only when the ground is wet. We can start tonight, at ten o'clock," Sherman said, his smile widening.

"I will show you how tonight, and then you are on your own from then on. I will give you the empty coffee cans, and I will take the worms to the stores for you, and we will split the money fifty-fifty. Deal?"

We shook hands on our new venture and agreed to meet in the backyard of the apartment at ten o'clock that night. I was on pins and needles the remainder of the day. Ten o'clock worked fine with my schedule since Mother worked the late shift, which ended after midnight, and Sister went to bed at nine o'clock on most nights.

I spent the balance of that long day waiting for nightfall. I began to worry when it did not rain that evening, remembering what Sherman had said about the worms coming out only after a rain. I also began to worry about how to find worms on the ground in a dark backyard.

My fears were abated when later that evening I saw Sherman using his hose to water the backyard grass. He also had laid two flashlights on the back porch steps.

At ten o'clock, I was waiting impatiently for Sherman. It was very dark with no moon. Sherman arrived and announced, "We have to get on our hands and knees and not make any noise." He handed me a flashlight, and he and I began crawling on all fours around his large, grassy, wet backyard. Sure enough, we soon found large, finger-size worms crawling out of their hidden holes into the thick, wet grass.

Amazingly, I soon learned how to rub the belly of a half-exposed worm and force him to release his death grip on his ground hole.

Our several coffee cans were soon full with masses of large, energetic, intertwined worms. Sherman put a handful of wet green moss on top of each full can of worms and covered it with a plastic cover with small holes.

Our first night produced about two hundred excellent worms, all in about thirty minutes. I was excited, wet, and muddy, and amazed at my new business. True to his word, Sherman took the worms to the local fishing stores the next day and handed me five dollars as my part of the earnings. I suspected that he gave more than half of the sale's proceeds, but I did not question him; after all, Mother always said, "Don't look a gift horse in the mouth," whatever that meant.

I was ready to harvest our worm crop every night, but Sherman said to only water the grass at six o'clock once a week to avoid depleting all the worms in his backyard. I suspected he was more concerned with his water bill. But at least I had a steady week's source of income.

And while my income was looking up, the same was not true for Mother. She complained long and loud about how she hated her waitress job. She never seemed happy with any job she ever had.

Now she worked from five o'clock until one o'clock in the morning. Since I was the man of the house, it was my responsibility to prepare dinner each night for Sister and me. It usually consisted of my favorite meal, peanut butter sandwiches for me, and peanut butter and grape jelly sandwiches for Sister.

Mother forbade Sister and me to leave the apartment for any reason. We had no friends, so we were bored out of our minds. Sherman gave us board games to play. That helped some. We had no radio, no pets, —no TV in those days. We were prisoners in our own home.

Sister and I would think up silly games to play. One game we created only lasted one night. We had noticed the constant stream of people walking by on the sidewalk outside our front living room window. We would stand for hours at night watching couples, young and old, hand in hand, walk by our window. We noticed that if we had the lights on in our apartment and our window shades pulled open, the people would see Sister and me with our noses to the front window and wave at us. We gladly waved back.

I came up with a plan one night to break out of our prison of boredom. I needed to enlist Sister's help since my plan would require two people. I instructed her in how our little game would work. She would stand in the corner of our front living room, holding the cord to our front window shade, which would be kept in a lowered position. Then, upon my verbal command, she would raise the window shade to the top and then immediately lower it again.

She practiced a few times, and when we were ready, I took all my clothes off and peeked through the window curtain until I saw a walking couple approaching the front of our yard. Then I stood in front of the window, completely nude, with arms and legs spread, and commanded Sister to raise and lower the window shade. Sister did so and then peeked out of the front window to see what had occurred. The first couple was laughing and pointing at our window as they hurriedly walked away. An older couple was approaching, so we repeated our little activity. But this time, the man came to our door and knocked loudly. We froze. He knocked several more times. We turned off all our lights in the house and stayed very quiet. He finally walked away, muttering something we could not understand. So much for that little game, so we returned to our board games.

The boredom became overwhelming after a few months, and since Mother had not enrolled us in school, we had nothing to do and no one to play with.

Sherman felt sorry for Sister and me since we went nowhere and had no friends. I told him Mother commanded us not to venture from our apartment. We watched longingly as the other neighborhood children played in their yards and at the nearby park grounds.

Mother took an instant dislike to Sherman; only she knew why.

Sister and I hid Sherman's board games from Mother because she never missed an opportunity to say bad things about him and his *money-grubbing* ways. Mother found our stash of board games and puzzles under our bed one day and was able to obtain a quick confession from Sister. She exploded in rage and scared the heck out of Sister and me. She stormed up to Sherman's apartment, and we could hear her screaming at Sherman and slamming doors. Mother took the board games and puzzles and piled them outside Sherman's front door.

I did not see or talk to Sherman for several days thereafter. Needless to say, my worm income stopped. Finally, I went to his door one night when Mother was at work. The door opened slowly. Sherman looked at me with a startled and somewhat uneasy expression.

"Why have you stopped talking to us, Sherman?" I pleaded, my eyes getting moist.

"Your mom threatened to call the police on me if I didn't stay away from you two kids. She said I was a dirty old man!"

"She goes nuts every now and then. She doesn't mean any harm. She would not call the cops on you," I lied. "Maybe if you would hire me as your handyman to sweep off the front porch and sidewalk each day, I could buy our own board games, and Mother would forgive you."

Sherman broke into a smile and said I was a real trooper and agreed to pay me five dollars per week, plus continue the once-a-week income from our worm business.

"You must clear this with your Mother first before I can even talk to you further about these matters," Sherman explained. I agreed.

I spoke that night to Mother. Her face immediately reddened, but before she spoke, I said, "If you do not agree, then you need to buy us some games and puzzles, because we are going crazy!" So she agreed.

So, at the ripe old age of nine, I was financially independent, making ten dollars per week and not having to ask for any money. This was to become a way of life for me. Thereafter, I never asked Mother for money again. If I did not earn it, I went without.

I bought board games, comic books, and puzzles for Sister and me, but soon we were bored to death again.

My little brain started to work overtime. Mother would not let Sister and I go to the movies, but she went out quite frequently herself. I thought of a solution to our isolation. We would go to the movies on the same nights Mother went out on a date. I had the money from my earnings that I could use to treat us to a movie. The only problem was timing everything exactly; there was no room for errors. The consequences would have been severe. Mother would never have agreed to such a night out for Sister and me.

The movie theater downtown started its double feature movies at about eight o'clock each night. The movies were usually over by midnight.

Sister and I caught the seven thirty evening bus at the end of our block and rode it until it reached downtown. Then we walked the one block to the movie theater.

Mother's new boyfriend was an engineer of some type. He was a very organized and predictable fellow. He always arrived at seven o'clock on Mother's date nights, and he always brought her home at one o'clock in the morning.

Sherman frequently rode the city bus to downtown and back and had given me a bus schedule.

At seven-thirty on those evenings, Sister and I caught the bus and traveled to the downtown bus station and walked to the nearby movie theatre. We always had to leave the theater at midnight in order to catch the last bus of the night returning to our street. We sometimes had to miss the last few minutes of a movie, but that was better than getting caught.

We usually had the same bus driver. He was more than a little curious about Sister and me riding the city bus at those hours. We did not see other children our ages. I think the driver knew what we were doing, but he just smiled and winked when we got on or off the bus. I would discuss the John Wayne moves with him, especially the war movies. Sister did not care for war movies, but she enjoyed the cartoons and popcorn.

Our movie routine continued until September, when school started.

Mother was afraid Sherman would report her to the authorities if she did not enroll us in the local schools, so I enrolled in the third grade while Sister started the second grade.

I immediately fell in love with my pretty dark-haired teacher. I think she liked me also since she would catch me staring at her in class and would wink at me and smile. I worked very hard on my schoolwork in an effort to impress my teacher. It was a struggle. I had missed many weeks of school during the trip to Vermont and back and certainly had no help at home, so I was very weak in reading, writing, and arithmetic.

Several times my teacher sent notes home to Mother to come to school for a conference, but Mother said she had more important things to worry about.

Besides my crush on my teacher, I discovered something else I had never encountered before: a playmate. His name was Billy. We were immediately inseparable from the day we met. His family had only recently moved to our area, and he was new to the school and lived near our apartment.

We would explore the neighborhood together each evening after school. We would put pennies on the railroad tracks and retrieve the flattened coins after the trains passed.

One day, Mother announced she wanted to "Meet this Billy" I was always talking about. She told me to invite him over to our apartment after school.

When I brought Billy to our apartment to meet Mother, she was standing on the front porch. She stared at Billy and then went into our apartment and slammed the door, never saying a word.

Later that night, she informed me to keep Billy away and to stay away from him. I was shocked.

"Why?"

"Because he is black—a nigger, you idiot. That's why!"

I learned for the first time that people of different skin color were not to be treated the same.

Billy and I drifted away from each other after that incident. He seemed to be uneasy around me.

Sister and I returned to our routine of entertaining ourselves any way we could. We talked about the movies we had seen and began planning to return to our movie night dates. That did not happen. Our lives were about to take another sharp corner.

———

CHAPTER 3
Oklahoma

• • •

EVERYTHING SUDDENLY CHANGED ONE NIGHT when Mother came home from one of her dates. She woke Sister and me from a deep sleep and loudly proclaimed, "We are moving! Get dressed and get packed, now."

I protested briefly, "What about our school? Why the need to move *right now*?"

She silenced my questions.

"Do not give me a hard time; just do as you are told. Get packed, now!"

I requested a minute to go tell Sherman good-bye. That was quickly denied.

"Don't tell that bastard anything. We owe him rent!"

We quickly packed our three suitcases, one big one and two smaller ones, and they were soon loaded in the Ford and we were heading down the Pacific Coast for California in total darkness and on wet highways in Bill's former Ford Coupe.

Mother never said why we had to leave so suddenly. The subject was not open for discussion. I suspected it had something to do with her boyfriend, since she had his billfold in her purse.

We drove to Sacramento, California, and stayed for a day in a motel. Mother was gone all day. She never said where she went or why we stopped.

She had the money she owed Sherman for last month's rent and also had her boyfriend's wallet and its contents.

Mother said she was not going to check Sister and me out of school because she did not want "those people" to know where we were going.

"We are going to go somewhere and start all over," was her announcement. "A new life, in a new place."

For the next three weeks, our little black Ford Coupe wandered all over the Western United States, stopping here and there for a day or two but never staying long.

One morning, while we were at a motel in a very dry desert city near Reno, Nevada, I discovered fire, sort of.

I was bored, Mother was gone, and I found a book of matches. A bored boy with matches is a dangerous thing. One of my lit matches touched the branches of a small pine tree in the parking lot, and it exploded in flames. I ran to the motel manager and screamed, "Fire!" and he was able to extinguish the fire with a hose before it did any real damage. When the fire department arrived, the firemen stated that spontaneous fires were starting everywhere due to the extreme dryness, and only our quick actions saved the community. Needless to say, I learned a lesson that day about fires and matches.

Mother was suspicious as to why I had been the first to spot the fire, but she had too much on her mind to worry about the details. I was glad that we checked out of the motel and hit the road before I was discovered as the culprit. I left the box of matches in the room.

After several weeks of aimless highway wandering, Mother finally announced her decision.

"We are going to live in Oklahoma, the place of my birth."

We drove east as fast as that Ford could move, loaded as it was with everything we owned.

I started to remember the Western movies Sister and I had seen concerning Oklahoma. Wasn't that where cowboys and Indians lived? As I remembered the Roy

Rogers and Gene Audrey movies of the Wild West, I began to get excited.

I had never seen a real horse or cow that I could remember. I began asking many questions.

"How far is it to Oklahoma? Are we going to live there a long time or move again?"

Mother was happier now that she had made the big decision. "Oklahoma will be our last move, I promise," she said.

"I am going home to stay; I am tired of running," Mother sighed, like a great weight was lifting from her shoulders.

"Running from what?" I inquired. "Are people still chasing us?" I was getting alarmed.

Mother ignored my questions and began describing her last contact with her home, Oklahoma.

"All my family lived in Oklahoma. They were sharecroppers working the fields. I ran away from home when I was sixteen—couldn't stand that life anymore.

"I am sure they are all dead now," she explained. "They probably worked themselves to death."

"Everyone?" I asked, a little puzzled.

"Yes, everyone," she replied.

"How do you know they have died?" I asked.

"I just do," she snorted at me for questioning her.

"All us kids had to work in the fields; we needed to work to keep food on the table. Times were tough. Ever heard of the Great Depression or Dust Bowl Days?"

I had to admit my lack of knowledge of those events.

"You mean you dropped out of school in the third grade, the same grade I am in now?" I asked in amazement; since I knew so very little about anything, it was amazing to me that she could survive in this world with only the education I had. So I was nine, and she was about forty-three, and we had the same education.

"Mother, are we going to have to work in the fields?" The thought suddenly sent chills down my back.

Mother looked at me and said, "A strong boy like you should be able to pull a hundred pounds of cotton a day. Work from sunup to sundown."

"That does not sound like very much fun," I mumbled.

"Fun!" She tightened her grip on the steering wheel and, looking straight ahead, stated, "You will soon learn to be a farm boy in Oklahoma."

I was starting to suspect our new life was going to be much different from our previous existence.

"Oklahoma has cowboys and Indians. Real Indians," Mother suddenly said. "Did you know your grandfather was a Cherokee chief?"

"Am I part Indian?" I yelled in amazement.

Mother smiled and nodded her head.

"Your father is full-blood Swede."

"Does that make me a half-breed?" I remembered that term from a Western movie.

"Probably," she replied. "More likely, white trash."

"What is that?" I asked.

"Oh, you will find out soon enough," she replied. "We will raise our own food, butcher our own beef, chickens, and pigs. We will never have to ask anyone for anything," Mother almost yelled.

"You know how to do all that?" I looked at her in amazement.

"Yep, that and more."

"Yeah, sure you can. You are kidding me. How do you butcher a pig?" I asked, thinking that would slow her down.

"Well, first you hang them by their rear legs from a tree, cut their throats, bleed them out, lower them into boiling water in an iron pot, and then raise them up. You scrape off all their hair and bristles and then cut them down the backbone into two halves and then cut the halves into hams, ribs, bacon, chops, and shoulders. Any more questions, Mr. Smarty?"

Sister let out a low moan from the back seat.

"Can you two talk about something else?" she said. "You are making me sick."

Mother was on a tear now. She continued, "Killing and butchering cattle is different. You have to skin them after you kill them. Then you must chill their meat immediately, unlike pork meat, which you can smoke or sugar cure. Of course, beef is much heavier and hard to handle and cut up into smaller pieces."

I was ready to change the subject, and Sister needed to stop and head for the bathroom, holding her mouth.

Mother was driving like a woman on a mission. It seemed like we drove for almost a week until we arrived in a small town in southeastern Oklahoma, about twenty miles from the Red River border with Texas.

Mother appeared to know the area, making comments to herself about various landmarks we passed.

She stopped at an old run-down motel on the outskirts of the town of Hugo, Oklahoma. The motel was really just a collection of twelve small cabins. The owner/manager of the place talked to Mother for a while, handed her a key, and pointed to one of the empty cabins, our new home. He smiled and waved to Sister and me sitting in the car. He looked at our Oregon license tags, shook his head, and walked back into his office. His expression matched my thoughts: "What in the world are those people doing here?"

We unpacked, and Mother said we would be living in the one-bedroom cabin for a week or so until she found us a farm to buy.

"Do you know anyone in this town?" I asked.

"Maybe," she replied. "Just don't worry about it." She acted like she was on some type of secret mission.

I questioned her about how she was going to buy a farm when we had no money. She replied, "You just let me worry about that."

There was only one big bed in the cabin, so it was deferred to Mother and Sister, and I staked out the small couch for my new bed.

Mother gave me five dollars and said to walk to the little store about a block away and buy some milk, bread, and eggs and put them in the small refrigerator in our cabin.

Mother announced, "I need to go see a man about a dog."

"A dog! What do we need a dog for?" I asked.

"That's just an old saying, telling someone to mind his or her own business," she replied.

I got the message. At least there was an old radio in the cabin, but it only received the local radio station that broadcasted from six in the morning to six in the evening. Soon, the radio was playing country songs, and Hank Williams was blaring with his strange, twangy voice.

I walked down the street to the store; a dog soon joined me, a shaggy white and brown shepherd. He looked like us, an orphan or something no one wanted.

He walked a short distance behind me with apprehension on his long-nosed face. I stopped and knelt down and called to him. He crawled on his belly to me. I petted his head and stroked his matted, dirty neck. He wagged his tail and jumped up and down, I was his master.

He walked close behind me as I resumed my trip to the store. The store manager stood in the door and shouted, "Don't let that mangy dog in my store. He will piss on everything."

The dog stopped in his tracks, seeming to know he was the subject of the conversation. He backed away and sat on his haunches.

"Whose dog is that?" I inquired.

"Someone dumped him a week ago, and he keeps trying to get inside; probably smells food," the manager explained.

I located the items Mother needed and paid for them, making sure the change was correct. Mother always said, "You can tell when a kid is mature and dependable if he brings you back the correct change from the store."

The manager handed me two cans of old dog food.

"You can have this dog food if you will take that dog home with you."

"Okay," I replied. So I did.

Butch wagged his tail so hard I thought it would break when I showed him the two cans of dog food. He followed the food and me back to our cabin. Butch seemed a good name for him since he reminded me of a comic book dog by that name and he seemed happy with it. I was excited to have a friend, and he was excited to have a family.

Butch wanted to come into the cabin with me, but that did not seem proper. So I found a can opener and gave him a can of dog food in an old soup bowl that was in the cabin. He inhaled the food, so I gave him a bowl of water to top off his meal.

There was a water faucet outside the cabins, probably to water the grass and plants since it had a water hose attached to it.

I found an old used bar of soap in our cabin and proceeded to give Butch a bath, probably his first. He was uneasy at first and then relaxed and enjoyed the attention.

"Good boy," I announced when we were finished. He promptly shook off the water and soaked me, so we both had a learning experience. He was so excited he ran circles around me until I stopped him with a bear hug.

"Butch, you are clean and happy now!"

I said this loud enough that Sister could hear. She came outside to see whom I was talking to.

"Mother will kill you," she said when she saw my new dog.

"No, she won't. This is a farm dog, trained and everything," I lied. "His name is Butch, and he is very smart," I explained.

We played chase until we were exhausted and lay on the grass together and bonded—a boy and his first dog.

When Mother returned several hours later, I showed her Butch, our new family member. She seemed uninterested.

"Keep him outside; we will be moving into our farm in about a week."

Sure enough, a week later, we loaded up the Ford, with an additional shaggy family member, and drove about four miles out of town into the countryside of pastures and thick woods and brush.

"There it is," Mother proudly proclaimed as we drove into the front yard of the old one-story frame house. The house reminded me of the outlaw houses in movies where the bad guys would hide from the sheriff's posse. The house certainly was a sight all right, with its sagging porch, roof, and missing shingles.

The house was certainly not the type of house or apartment we had lived in before.

I looked at Sister, and she looked at me with looks of misgiving.

Butch was fine with the place and immediately started to check out the several outbuildings.

"What are those other buildings?" I asked, pointing at the small buildings behind our house and what looked like an old barn about half a block behind our house.

"That one is the outhouse, where you use the bathroom," Mother pointed to the smaller building. "The large building farther back is our barn, for cattle and horses, when we get some."

Mother unlocked the front door, and we walked inside to see our new home. It already had old furniture in it. There was a double bed and one dresser in the larger bedroom, and a single bed and no dresser in the small bedroom. Beyond the bedrooms, I could see an old refrigerator and a two-burner electric stove. There was one worn couch in the living room with a cheap dinette and four wobbly chairs. No fireplace, but a naked stove pipe appeared in the ceiling of the larger bedroom. There was no indoor plumbing, only a sink in the kitchen that drained directly into the backyard under the kitchen window. After a brief walk-through of the one-story frame house, I noticed with alarm that there were no bathrooms or water in the house. A single light bulb with a string attached hung from the center ceiling of each room. It had no outlets or light switches.

"Where are the water faucets?" I asked.

"There are none. Water is in the well, outside."

Mother looked away and walked to examine the few kitchen cabinets.

"How do you get water into the house?" I asked.

"Just pull it up with the bucket at the end of the chain. Very simple."

Mother opened the back door and pointed in the direction of the water well in the backyard.

"So how do you take a bath in cold water?" I asked.

"You warm it up in a pan on the stove and pour it into a washtub and climb in and wash yourself, silly," Mother explained, a little annoyed.

Sister had overheard these comments and softly asked, "So where do you take a bath?"

"In that metal washtub hanging on the back porch," Mother explained.

I walked out on the back porch, which creaked and felt very unsteady under my feet, and inspected the metal washtub hanging on a hook on the side of the porch. It was about two feet wide and three feet long. It looked more like a water trough for animals than a human bathtub.

Butch sat patiently on his hind legs near the back porch, waiting to inspect the area and the out buildings behind the house. The backyard was full of tall weeds and grass. Off to one corner was a large, black, wrought iron pot, which looked like it had been used to heat water in, since its sides were black with soot and it sat on a bed of old ashes.

"Let's go explore, Butch," I hollered, and off we ran.

First stop was the chicken shed located between the back of our house and the large barn. The shed had a slanted roof and was a little smaller than a carport. I jerked open the door, half expecting chickens to scatter, and stepped into the chicken-feces smelling interior, Butch at my heels.

I focused my eyes in the dark to discover I was staring into the face of a large, full-grown raccoon sitting on a head-high shelf. He suddenly reared up on his hind legs and showed his teeth and hissed like a snake.

Butch went crazy, jumping and barking at the raccoon. I grabbed Butch by the neck, and we backed out of the shed and quickly closed the door.

I ran to the car to get my rifle, swearing to never be without it again around this place. I retrieved and checked the rifle to make sure it was loaded, grabbed some more .22 shells, and ran back to the shed.

I slowly opened the door with one hand, holding Butch back with the other. The raccoon was gone. We found his escape tunnel under the back wall of the shed.

Next, Butch and I inspected the smelly outdoor toilet, more often referred to as an *outhouse*. It was a one-holer, which emptied into a dug-out hole in the ground about three feet below the seat. I wondered whose responsibility it was to clean that mess. I did not even want to think about it. It was well stocked with green flies and old Sears catalogs.

Butch and I ran to the barn and walked into a large, dirt-floored, two-story, oak log and wooden plank building that consisted of several stalls, a feeding trough area, and hayloft. It also had many rats that scattered when we entered. I was afraid to shoot them since I needed rat-shot shells to kill the rodents, not the lead bullets I had, which might have ricochet back from the oak boards and posts and done great damage to Butch and me instead of the rats.

"We'll get 'em later, Butch," I instructed. He seemed to understand perfectly.

Butch and I proceeded back to the house and looked down into the water well. Sure enough, the water reflected my image. It appeared to be about twenty-five feet to the water. A metal water bucket hung over the center of the wheel from the supporting poles and was equipped with a pulley and long chain.

I lowered the bucket until it sunk in the water and then pulled the chain until the bucket was within reach. It held about one gallon of cool water, and the bucket unsnapped so it could be carried into the house. This was my first experience with a working water well.

It dawned on me that we had traveled back in time probably thirty or forty years to the time when Mother was a child. Now I understood. She was home again, after over thirty years of running, running from many unknown demons.

Wow, I thought, this was going to be a completely different world from what I had known.

Mother and Sister were unpacking our suitcases and trying to clean the dirty old house when I walked back inside.

"How much land do we have?" I asked.

"Forty acres," Mother replied.

I had no idea how much land that was.

"How do you know what land is yours?"

"It is all within one barbed-wire fence. Just walk around inside the fence, and when you have walked clear around the property you will be back where you started. It is a quarter of a mile on each side, a perfect square," she explained.

"There is a stock tank in the center of the property, probably full of fish," she continued.

"What is a stock tank?" I asked.

"It is a large pond of water for the livestock to drink."

With those words about fishing, I grabbed my rifle and Butch, and we set off to walk the fence. It took us an hour to circle the property, and then we went to inspect the pond of water.

Butch jumped in and swam in big circles, showing off. A pair of black birds chased him out of the water when he came too close to their nest.

I walked back into the house and asked Mother where she got the money to buy a farm. She ignored me and said, "None of your business. Just be glad you have it."

I would spend the next several weeks exploring the woods and pastures surrounding our farm.

There were also several abandoned houses and barns nearby, all that was left from the Dust Bowl days when many of the Okies had fled to California in the thirties and forties to seek a new life. Some, like Mother, had fled this area when younger, only to return in later life. She was home, but I had doubts this would ever be *home* to Sister and me.

———

CHAPTER 4
Country Schooling

• • •

THERE WERE NO ONE PARENT families living in our area. A single woman in her mid-forties with young children meant trouble to the local married women, who wanted nothing to do with Mother. Most married men also found themselves uncomfortable dealing with Mother. Sister and I lied to our nosy teachers and neighbors who inquired about *our father's whereabouts*, stating, "Our father is dead," and hinting he had been in the military to give the appearance of misfortune rather than the image of a family abandoned.

Our standing in the community took an even greater step down when Mother started receiving a state welfare check in the mail each month. News traveled quickly in our small community. Mother did not work, so that did not help, since in this part of the country, parents either worked for a living or were considered deadbeats. And like most deadbeats, we immediately qualified for a free supply of commodities given away to needy families by the state welfare office.

Our monthly box of peanut butter, canned meat, dried eggs, milk, flour, cornmeal, and Velveeta cheese soon became the staples of our diet and a further embarrassment to Sister and me, who had to attend the monthly ritual of standing in line at the welfare office. The welfare office demanded proof from Mother that we were enrolled in school, so she now had to get serious about our schooling. She had two choices of schools since we lived between two separate school district boundaries. We could go to the local Hugo public schools or the rural country school.

The city school was three miles south of our place, the country school ten miles north. A school bus provided transportation to the country school or to the city school. It was up to the parents which school their children attended. Mother enrolled us in the country school. I noticed that all our neighbor's children went to the city schools and very few rode the bus. I wondered why.

The country school looked like a country school: one large, one-story red building divided into six classrooms by wall partitions. The only other room in the building was a coatroom, where everyone hung their coats, umbrellas, and rubber boots. It was always a mess.

There were no bathrooms in the building. The bathrooms were in an out-building with separate boys and girls' entrances. It had running water and working toilets.

Six teachers taught their respective classes, five women and a male sixth grade teacher-principal. He only had one arm. He was a veteran of World War II.

It was obvious from the first day of school that discipline was a real problem at this school. The principal always carried a hickory paddle with him everywhere, and he used it freely on unruly kids' bottoms. His one arm was very strong, and the sounds of paddle licks echoed frequently throughout the school building, followed by moans or crying.

Sister and I felt uneasy from the start of our enrollment. We did not fit in with these country kids, many of who were repeating the same grades for the second and third time, many with no success.

I was enrolled in the third grade, Sister in the second. This was not the type of school we had attended before.

Sister and I had never seen or heard of paddling students, but we soon learned that was the only way to control some of the oversized kids.

Going to the country school was more about *survival* than learning. Each school day was filled with threats and physical contact between students. Sister stayed close to me when she was not in class. She was really scared, and we made no friends.

Most of the school children came from homes whose parents had never gone to school themselves and really saw no need for a child's education. After all, you don't need an education to saw logs or till the field or tend to livestock.

Education did not seem to be an overriding concern to the teachers at the school, either. Maintaining order was their utmost chore. I complained to Mother about the conditions in the rural school and how Sister and I were fearful and were not learning anything. She just shrugged and ignored me.

"Nothing I can do. You have to go to school," she said. "Otherwise our checks will stop, and we will starve."

Our school experience got worse by the day. The daily classes ended at three-thirty each afternoon, but the school buses did not arrive from the city until four-thirty. That one-hour with two hundred out-of-control kids became an ordeal each day.

The five women teachers bailed out of the school as soon as the bell sounded, leaving the principal to close down everything. He was the only person left to maintain any order. Sister and I soon identified the troublemakers in the school and tried to avoid them as much as possible. We tried to become invisible.

Two older boys in particular always caused trouble. They were both fifth graders who had repeated their grade several times. They were twin brothers, Jimmy and Johnny. They were the ringleaders of the rougher kids and were constantly in some type of trouble. Johnny was larger than his brother, but Jimmy was the leader, both in brains and loudness.

I knew the twins were watching Sister and me each day, and they would point and shout and laugh at us to impress their followers. We ignored them. I felt for sure that trouble was going to occur between the twins and us before long.

I noticed that one of the girls in my class had tears in her eyes when she boarded the homebound bus one evening. I overheard her telling her girlfriend that Jimmy and Johnny had *coatroomed* her. I was not sure what that meant, but it did not sound appealing. It was common knowledge in the school that the school coatroom was where certain bad things occurred after the teachers left school in the afternoon and the students took charge of the grounds.

A week later, while Sister and I waited for the afternoon bus to arrive at the school, Jimmy and Johnny and several of their cohorts walked up to Sister and stated, "Come with us to the coat room. We have a surprise to show you." They ignored me.

Sister froze, and I stepped between her and them.

"Leave her alone," I said.

Everyone around stopped and stared. I had never been in a fight before and did not really know what to do next. But I was the man of the house and needed to protect Sister somehow.

Johnny shoved me aside, and he and Jimmy each grabbed one of Sister's arms and pulled her toward the school building. Pure panic was in her eyes, but she never said a word. All the other students watched and waited. I ran after them and gathered all my strength and drove my right fist as hard as I could into Jimmy's stomach. He yelled and stumbled, letting go of Sister and holding his stomach as he went to his knees.

Johnny whirled around and grabbed both my arms from behind and flung me to the ground. I looked up to see his left shoe headed for my face. I rolled on the ground like my life depended on it. Johnny yelled at the same time, and I heard the principal's hickory paddle make contact with his backside.

Jimmy and Johnny walked away quickly. The one-armed principal stood there ready to administer more punishment if needed. He winked to me and said, "You two need to stay close to me after school from now on until your bus arrives. Those twins are not going to leave you guys alone."

When sister and I arrived home that night, I announced to Mother, "We will not return to that horrible school. We will walk to the city school each day before we will return to that place!"

Mother must have believed me because the next day she enrolled us in the city school, and we made arrangements to ride the rural bus each morning to the rural school and switch to the city-bound bus.

Each day, Jimmy and Johnny stood on the school grounds of the country school and watched us make our bus transfer. They would freely make comments and gestures to us. I knew I had not seen the last of the twins. Several months later, the school expelled them.

I was struggling with my third grade school work now that I was enrolled in the better city school. Sister was struggling, also. We both had missed too many school days while we had toured the country.

One spring day, my teacher asked me for Mother's telephone number. We did not have a phone. I suspected the worst, and I was correct. The teacher gave me a sealed note to take to Mother, which I did.

"What have you done?" Mother asked after reading the note. "The principal wants a conference with me tomorrow."

It only got worse the next day when Mother drove Sister and me to school and all three us walked to the principal's office. The principal looked at Mother.

"Ma'am, your two children missed more days of school than they attended this last school year. They are both struggling to catch up with their classmates. They both need to repeat their grades."

A chill ran down my neck. I felt light-headed. Sister and I would not only be outsiders, but now we would also be labeled as dummies, a fate worse than death.

Mother was not surprised by the horrid news and agreed with the principal. It was only a week from the end of the school year anyway, so the principal excused us from having to finish that last week of school.

We quietly returned home with Mother, sad and very embarrassed at the thought of having to return to school in the fall and be in classes with new kids and having to face the questions and stares of our former classmates on the schoolyard.

Sister and I had never finished an entire school year at the same school prior to this date. Our education was not an important part of our lives. Sister and I could not read or write very well, as our teachers frequently pointed out to us. Except for a few comic books and cereal boxes, there was nothing to read around the house, anyway, so I really did not see the need to learn something I did not use.

We had certainly not gotten off to a good start in our new home.

———

CHAPTER 5
A New Lifestyle

• • •

OUR FIRST SUMMER IN OKLAHOMA was a lonely time for Sister and me. We lived in a sparsely populated area with the farmhouses scattered, usually sitting on 160 acres of land and spaced out about one-half-mile apart. Most of the people who lived on our dusty dirt road were related to each other. It was not unusual for three generations of families to live within a mile of each other on their separate farms. There were some large ranches in the area consisting of hundreds of acres, but most of those ranchers actually lived in the city and just drove out occasionally to check on their fences and livestock.

The first summer was my time to explore all those large ranches and their broad woods and pastures. Most of the ranchers did not care if people crossed their properties as long as they did no damage to the fences or livestock.

Sister was afraid of the deep woods, so she always stayed close to the house. I would arise at dawn and eat some scrambled eggs made with powdered eggs and powered milk, prepare a peanut butter sandwich, grab my rifle and Butch, and head for the woods. We would roam all day and explore the pastures, the creeks, the hills, and the abandoned houses and barns.

One day, while roaming the woods a mile or so from my home, a voice from nowhere startled me.

"Any luck?"

I whirled around to see a boy about my size leaning against a large pecan tree, virtually invisible in his dark tan clothes.

"Oh, hi there. You startled me. I am Bobby."

"George here," he replied and walked over to where I stood. George said he lived about one mile away, on a different road. He was home-schooled by his mother, so he did not go to any of the local schools, which explained why I had never seen him before.

He related how he loved the woods and exploring and knew all the good fishing and swimming holes around the area.

He was a year older than me and had moved to this area two years earlier from the *great state of Texas*. His father was a logging contractor and hauled hardwood logs to local sawmills. His mother was a *Bible thumper* and made him and his younger brother, who was my age, go to church each Sunday. He had two hours of home-schooling each morning, and then after that, he was free and would grab his bolt-action .22 Remington repeating rifle and take to the woods to spend the remainder of daylight.

This was all music to my ears. I asked quietly and held my breath, "Maybe we can meet every day in these woods and you can show me the fishing and swimming holes?"

He was as excited as me. "Sure. I haven't made any friends since we moved here, so that would be great! Can you shoot that thing?" He pointed at my short-barreled single-shot rifle. "Why is the barrel so short? Never seen a .22 with such a short barrel."

"Long story," I replied and pointed at his rifle.

"This is my dad's gun, but he lets me use it." He handed me his rifle.

I had never handled a repeating rifle. Each time you opened the bolt, it ejected the spent shell and loaded a new bullet into the chamber; pretty neat.

"Holds sixteen shells," George proudly announced. "I can hit a penny dead center at fifty feet. Can you?"

"Never tried," I said, "But I am pretty good myself. Okay, let's see."

George pointed at a small sumac sapling about fifty feet away, about the diameter of a finger. "I will shoot that sumac into two pieces."

He aimed and fired. The sapling jerked but still stood straight. The bullet had hit the sapling a little off-center, leaving the stalk held up by half its width.

I raised my rifle, aimed, and fired. The sumac fell, my bullet completing the final separation of the sapling.

"Wow." George was impressed.

"What a team."

We bonded, and from that day forward, almost daily, except for Sundays, George and I met, and he taught me to be a country boy: how to hunt rabbits and squirrels, how to fish with nothing but a string and hook. But even more important, I learned how to love the freedom of nature and to protect the creatures of the woods and pastures. He became my best friend.

We only killed what we could clean and eat. We never killed just for the sake of killing, except for crows and blue jays. They ate other birds' eggs and sometimes their babies in the nests.

George taught me never to kill game animals in the spring or summer because that was when they raised their young. To kill an animal during those months meant their young in the nests would starve and die.

He taught me how to clean squirrels, rabbits, game birds, and fish. I was soon putting meat on our dinner table, which was much better than that canned meat.

I was soon supplying our dinner table with rabbit and squirrel meat in the winter months and fish in the spring and summer months.

Butch became our hunting guide. Butch was a quick study and very smart. We had a *connection*. He soon learned what game animals we were hunting on a particular day and focused his attention on finding those particular animals. "Squirrels" meant squirrels; "rabbits" meant rabbits; "birds" became quail. One day it might be rabbits and the next day squirrels, and the next day quail hunting.

One winter day, Butch surprised us both when we shot a mallard duck out of the sky and Butch jumped in the pond and swam through the icy water and returned with the duck in his mouth. The dog could do anything.

There were many types of snakes around our area, some harmless, some deadly. There were fast black snakes and blue racers, and aggressive and mean-spirited cottonmouth water moccasins and diamond-back rattlers.

Often, when walking through the deep woods or high green grass pastures, we would see a shadow move near our legs and we would stop and back away and call Butch. He would creep up to the hidden snake, and we could tell by the sound of his bark if it was a poisonous snake or harmless. He had a sharp, high-pitched, excited bark for the rattlers, moccasins, and copperheads. But for the harmless snakes, he would bark a few times and walk away. He could tell by the snake's smell what type it was. We learned to keep one eye on the ground at all times when we roamed the woods and pastures. The last thing we wanted to do was step on a poisonous snake, because it would immediately react by striking your foot or leg in self-defense.

Butch learned not to stick his head into hollow logs one day when a copperhead got him in the neck. We shot the snake, but a day later, Butch's neck was very swollen, and he was sick for a week. He recovered, but with a new respect for snakes in hollow logs.

We located several swimming and fishing holes in the creeks that flowed through the countryside. We would fish for a while, and if the fish were not biting, we just took off our clothes and dove into the cool waters and enjoyed ourselves immensely. We were Tom Sawyer and Huckleberry Finn. We had not a care in the world.

———

CHAPTER 6
Boredom

• • •

MOTHER GREW BORED after a few months and obtained a part-time waitress job at a dancehall lounge about twenty miles from our place. It was near the Red River, the border with Texas.

Mother explained to Sister and me that she could work on the weekend nights for cash and it would not jeopardize her welfare status.

Texas was dry, Oklahoma wet, so the thirsty Texas workers with cash in their jeans flooded the Oklahoma borderline lounges and dancehalls on weekend nights.

Although Mother was not supposed to work and collect welfare assistance, she understood the rules in this area of this world. Good God-fearing people did not go to bars and dancehalls. Therefore, no state welfare worker was going to report Mother for working in such a place. We lived in the Bible Belt region of Oklahoma where *the good* tried to avoid contamination by association with *the bad.*

People who worked in bars and dancehalls were not considered to be God-fearing and therefore were members of the shadow world of those with low moral standards. Once branded as a member of this lower class, it did not wash off.

Except for her weekend night jobs at the borderline lounges, Mother just sat around the house during the day. At least that is what she told us.

When we were home, Mother talked constantly about how the men in her life only used her and then abandoned her. She had no other topics of interest. The names changed, but the stories were always the same. Men would use her and then leave her with nothing, and this pattern had repeated all her life since she was sixteen.

I tried to be comforting, and I did not say much to her, but from my own recollection, Mother was the one always running from the men.

Mother saved her most extreme language and hatred for our father, "that sorry bastard," who abandoned her to raise Sister and me by herself.

The venom in her voice and hatred in her eyes when she spoke of our father was unnatural and scary. She often said, "I would kill the bastard with my bare hands if I could get my hands on him."

Mother probably could, too. She was very physically strong and stout as a man.

She was a well-built woman with attractive facial features, black hair and a straight Indian nose. She had an olive complexion and stood about five feet five. She also had a beautiful handwriting ability, a common trait of the local Indians, and that made me question her claims to only a third grade education.

I assumed Mother just sat around the house doing nothing when Sister and I were in school, since she sure did nothing to improve our living conditions. She seemed quite content with our lifestyle. She even started talking to herself quite frequently, something I had never noticed before. Sister and I would just walk out of the kitchen and leave her sitting at the table, talking about the "sorry-ass men" she had been forced to deal with over the years.

I began noticing that several of the neighborhood men would honk or wave when they drove past our house on that dusty, dirty road. I wondered how Mother had come to know them. I also noticed the men did not honk or wave if they had their wives or children in their vehicles. I also began to notice tire tracks in our dirt driveway that did not match our Ford Coupe. Mother had daily visitors, whom she did not care to speak about.

Since several of the neighboring men who honked and waved were carpenters or plumbers, I wondered why we had the only house on our road with no plumbing or running water.

In addition to the lack of plumbing, the front and back porches were rotting. Those items never seemed to be of much importance to Mother. It was just a matter of time before one of us fell through the porch.

One of the family-owned sawmills on our daily school bus route caught my interest. I noticed a large stack of boards about the size needed to repair our front and back porches. The stack of sawmill boards did not seem to be of any interest to the owner since that lumber appeared to be rejects from the neat piles of lumber that were for sale to the public.

One morning when the teenage boy who was a member of the sawmill family climbed on our bus, I asked him, "What are you going to do with that pile of lumber?" I pointed to the stack as the bus drove away.

"It has too many knot holes; we will probably just make firewood out of it."

"How much would you charge to sell it and deliver it to my house?" I asked.

"Ten dollars, cash money," was his quick reply.

"Deal," I said. "When can you deliver it?"

He agreed to have his older brothers deliver it that weekend.

All I needed now was a hammer and nails, and I could repair and replace our front and back porches before one of us fell through the rotting boards.

That night I proudly announced to Mother my purchase of the scrap lumber and my plans to repair the two porches.

"What? You are not a carpenter," Mother said. "Where do you think we are going to get ten dollars?"

I had saved ten dollars from my former business dealings in Oregon, and at nine years old, I was sure I could drive nails.

"Mother, I will pay for the lumber. You just get me an old hammer and some nails from one of your *friends* next time you get the chance."

She just turned away, shaking her head and muttering to herself about the mess I was going to make.

Several days later, an old hammer, a dull handsaw, and a sack of ten-penny nails appeared.

I immediately attacked my porch repair project with a flourish, measuring boards and ripping out the rotten pine one-by-fours and thankfully finding good oak supports underneath to attach the new boards to when they arrived.

I was waiting impatiently Saturday morning for the two older teenage brothers when they drove up in an old flatbed truck and hurriedly dumped out the purchased lumber in our yard.

One of the boys looked at my porch project and turned to me and asked, "You ever work with cured oak boards before?" He looked concerned.

"Well, no, I haven't. Is that a problem?" I asked.

"Yeah, it sure is, unless you have tempered steel nails. Normal nails will not work and will just bend. Oak boards are hard as concrete."

I realized the nails I had were not strong enough for such work.

"Any suggestions?" I asked, lacking the money to buy the more expensive nails that were needed.

"Yeah, get a bar of soap, wet the point of your nail, and stick its point into the bar of soap before you nail it into these oak boards."

He was correct; the soaped nails penetrated the oak boards, whereas the unsoaped nails simply bent over when struck with my hammer. And while my finished porch repair project was far from professional, at least we did not have to worry about falling through the rotting porch after I finished.

It was becoming apparent to me that I was not only Mother and Sister's designated protector; I was also now the only one around who was ever going to upgrade our living conditions.

———

CHAPTER 7
Wood Gathering

• • •

THAT FIRST WINTER, WE ALMOST froze. Mother had forgotten how cold Oklahoma winters could be, and she thought the one old wood-burning cook stove she had installed in her and Sister's bedroom was enough to warm our entire house. It was not.

My bedroom was like an icebox at nighttime. I would bury myself under heavy surplus army blankets and old cotton quilts. There was an open doorway between my smaller bedroom and the larger bedroom where Mother and Sister slept, but the heat from the wood stove in their room never seemed to make it through that doorway.

Mother filled the stove with firewood at night and turned down the stovepipe damper so that the fire burned slowly throughout the night. But a slow-burning fire does not create much heat.

We also learned that not all types of firewood create the same levels of heat. The firewood that Mother had purchased for the wood stove was oak, which makes good firewood but only if it has been dried for a year or so. Otherwise, it burns poorly and with a lot of smoke. The deal Mother got on the firewood was no deal. After freezing for a month trying to burn green firewood and breathing a great deal of smoke, Mother said we would simply harvest our own dried oak wood from our bottomland.

We had several old oak trees that had died on the rear potion of our forty acres, but they were in a wet marshy area where a truck would surely get stuck.

Mother decided to borrow a team of horses and a wagon from one of our neighbors, and we would load up the wagon with fallen dead oak tree limbs and haul the limbs back to our backyard and saw them into firewood as needed for our wood stove.

A few days later, when Sister and I got off the school bus, there was Mother standing in our front yard with a team of two horses already hooked up to a wagon.

"Let's go get some firewood, Bobby," she said and climbed into the wagon's front seat, holding the horse reins in her hands.

"You know how to handle horses?" I asked, a little concerned.

"Sure, I was raised driving a team of horses."

I climbed into the side chair next to Mother, and off we went into our woods. When the horses reached the marshy area, they became obviously nervous and hesitant to proceed into the muddy area.

Mother hollered at them and slapped their backsides with the reins. The horses walked slowly into the wet ground and into chest-high brush and finally stopped, their ears pointed skyward, and their heads jerked up and down nervously. They refused to take another step. Mother's hollering and slapping them with the reins was having no effect.

"Bobby, go down and walk in front of them so they can see that there is nothing to be afraid of in front of them," Mother ordered.

I leaped down from the wagon and walked around the two uneasy horses, and when I was in front of them, I saw what the problem was. Directly in front of their legs were several knee-high tree stumps that the horses did not want to pass.

I jumped up on the stumps to show Mother what the problem was. Mother pulled back on the reins to get the horses to back up, and that proved to be a big mistake. The horses panicked and reared up on their hind legs and ran directly over me. I was knocked down off the stumps, and the panicked horses and the wagon ran directly over me. My entire left arm was caught in the spokes of one of the passing wagon wheels. I screamed in agony. It felt like my left arm was being ripped from my body. The next thing I knew, my left arm was hanging useless to my side, pieces of white bone protruding from my twisted elbow. I lost feeling in that arm below the elbow. I could not stand up, but I managed to prop myself up in a sitting position on the same stump that had caused all the mess.

The wagon and team of horses stopped when they got stuck in the mud a short distance away.

I looked up when I heard voices coming from above me and saw Mother and the man she borrowed the horses from standing over me. I never knew where he came from, probably attracted by my screaming. Both their faces were white as sheets. I was covered in blood and mud and looked like road-kill.

The man spoke first. "We have got to get him to a hospital, quick."

With that, he picked me up like a baby and carried me to the nearest road.

The next thing I remember, I was in an ambulance, for a long time, a very long time, with an attendant looking down at me.

Upon my arrival at the local city hospital, the doctor on duty took one look at me and told the ambulance crew to take me to the state hospital in Ada, Oklahoma, over an hour away.

By the time we arrived in Ada, my left arm had swollen to three times its normal size. The arm was put in traction above my head for two weeks, until the swelling subsided. I could tell by the looks of the hospital staff when they examined my arm that there was a question about whether they could save it.

After two weeks of traction, a series of three elbow operations took place slowly putting the pieces of broken bone, muscle, and nerves back together. I was heavily sedated most of the time, but I remember that the nurses told me that Mother would return for me when I was ready to go home.

Clouds of loneliness settled over me after weeks of lying on my back while my left arm dangled from the overhead sling. I had no visitors. That all changed when a naked teenage boy was wheeled into my room.

His entire body was burned from head to toe. Nothing but wet tissues covered him, and they were changed hourly.

His body was losing all its life giving fluids. His parents stayed by his bedside as his life and death struggle unfolded in front of my eyes. I realized how fortunate I was and felt guilty for my earlier depression.

The teenager was heavily sedated and his father and I began passing time with conversations of my background and adventures. He was concerned with my lack of visitors, but I assured him Mother had to take care of our farm animals.

I managed to summons the courage when his wife was gone one day to ask him what happened to his son.

"Jerry had obtained a weekend job working at a Service Station near our home; his first job. He overfilled a customer's gas tank and the gasoline blew back and splattered him good. After the customer drove away he washed his hands and arms and went back to work. Sometime later, when no customers were there he was flicking open a cigarette lighter he found on the ground and his clothes erupted in flames. He panicked and ran screaming until a man tackled him and smothered the flames with his overcoat. That stranger saved my son's life."

I made a mental note about the dangers of gasoline fumes.

Jerry improved slowly and was moved to a private room and I never saw him or his parents again. His father did give me a parting gift, a Mr. Potato Head.

I played with that thing for days, amusing the staff. Other than that, I was alone. At least I was warm for three weeks.

It would take me almost a year to recover the use of my left arm. I worked out daily, lifting a bucket full of water with that mangled arm until it gained strength and size and looked like a match to my right arm.

I had been blessed with very good doctors who saved my left arm and a kind stranger who cared about a lonely boy, but more problems were on my horizon!

———

CHAPTER 8
Awakenings

• • •

AFTER SEVERAL YEARS IN OUR rural Oklahoma home, life settled into a routine of sorts.

Mother stayed home except on weekend nights, when she worked at the borderline lounges. She seemed content to entertain her male friends during the day while Sister and I were in school, and then hold her nightly kitchen table meetings about the evils of men and their double-crossing ways.

Sister grew even more into herself. She was a loner at school and preferred to stay around our house, playing with the calves and farm animals we were slowly accumulating. I always rode next to her on the morning and evening school bus so that the other kids did not pester her or make fun of her awkwardness around people. I would ask her to accompany Butch and me on our journeys to the creeks and swimming holes, but she would decline.

Mother discouraged Sister and me from any social contact with other children or with our neighbors, so we became hermits of a sort. George and Butch were my only non-school friends.

Mother often declared loudly, "We only need *each other*; everyone else can go to hell!" Therefore, Sister and I found ourselves without any social network, and we seemed to have no relatives with whom to communicate or socialize.

I asked Mother, "Where are all your family members? You said you were raised around here and yet we have never met anyone from either side of your family."

Mother would shrug her shoulders and walk away, not wanting to discuss anything about her family. It was all a big mystery to me as to why we would move ourselves across the country so Mother could return *home*, and there was no one home.

"Where is my Cherokee chief grandfather?" I asked.

"Dead," Mother said, declining any more discussion on that subject.

Mother was not much for learning, and at that point in my life, neither was I.

By the time I entered fifth grade, I was really struggling with my three R's. Mother never volunteered to help with our homework, and when asked, she reminded us she dropped out of school in third grade. She showed no interest in reading. The only reading material around was the Sears, Roebuck, & Co. catalogs in our outhouse. I did read its pages with interest on many occasions, mostly about sporting and farming equipment.

Everything changed for me when I stepped into Mrs. Stewart's fifth grade class. This was a teacher like I had never seen before. She was in her late fifties, tall, with gray hair. An "old farm girl," she freely declared.

She carried a two-foot chalkboard pointer stick with her at all times, and she used it effectively. *No one* slept in her class. She roamed up and down the aisles and around the room, determined during class to pound some learning into our hard heads.

If a student was daydreaming or not paying attention, she would walk up to the student's desk and slam down that pointer on the desk so hard that everyone in the class would jump.

The class had the multiplication tables memorized within short order. We would write until our hands and fingers gave out. We would read until our vision was blurred. She would have made an excellent Marine drill sergeant.

I was used to my third and fourth grade teachers giving students reading or writing assignments, and then the teachers laid their heads down on their desks and took a nap while the students supposedly did their schoolwork. Not a high-stress environment.

Mrs. Stewart was very different; she was not going to let anyone out of her class who did not know their three R's. I really had to listen, read, write, and do my math; otherwise, I would have the embarrassment of a pointer slamming down on my desk.

But a strange thing happened: the more I learned, the more I enjoyed learning. One day, as the class bell sounded, Mrs. Stewart asked me to stay and talk to her about farming, a subject she loved to discuss. After all the students had left, she told me, "You are my special student."

I blushed for fear that such a label would make me an outcast to the other students.

"I have been teaching for almost thirty years, and I know special students when I see them. They are few and far between, believe me! Bobby, you are one of those students," she continued, and I listened in anticipation.

"I know from talking to your other teachers that you have struggled since you started here, but you have that special something that sets you apart. Do not let your current situation at home and lack of money hold you back. You have a great future ahead of you."

My face was red as a beet, and I was looking down at the floor, unsure as to what to say in reply.

"Thank you, Mrs. Stewart."

"Bobby," she continued, "Have you ever gone to the city library down the street?"

"No, ma'am," I replied, trying to remember if I even knew about the library's existence.

"I want you to walk down to that library every Friday during your lunch hour and check out a library book to read over the weekend. Bring it back every Monday morning and show it to me. I want to see how many books you can read during this school year, okay?"

"Yes, ma'am."

I took the challenge. I started with the Hardy Boys mysteries. After that, I read all the Nancy Drew mysteries, and then I started reading the biographies of all the United States presidents and all the American generals.

Mrs. Stewart had awakened a voracious reader and learner. My thoughts began to focus on my long-term career plans and hopes for a better life in the future.

My fellow students were a little jealous of the closeness that developed between the teacher and me. I guess her constant remarks that I was the only farm boy in her class who knew the difference between a plow and a harrow had something to do with their jealousy. I certainly had changed over the last several years. I was no longer the boy from the West Coast who knew nothing about farming, hunting, or the outdoors. I was now a skilled woodsman and crack shot who could put meat on the table when the need arose. I loved to spend every waking hour exploring the creeks, hills, and pastures, looking for adventure.

I had become a real country boy in mind and spirit.

———

CHAPTER 9

Income

• • •

THERE WERE FEW JOBS AVAILABLE for anyone in our area of the world, and even fewer opportunities for a boy my age to earn money.

One day as I sat fishing on the earthen dam of our farm pond, I noticed large schools of shiny minnows working the surface of the pond, looking for food. I threw a handful of cracker crumbs into the water, and a feeding frenzy of jumping minnows erupted. The pond was full of the type of minnows that fishermen were buying in local bait shops. I remembered my days in Oregon and the night crawler business.

I ran a mile to a neighbor's house. I knew the brothers living there owned a ten-foot minnow seine, which they used to catch baitfish in nearby creeks.

One brother and I returned with the seine and waded out into our pond and stretched out the ten-foot length of the seine, swept it into a small corner of the pond, and dragged it out of the water.

The seine was full of minnows, hundreds of small, shiny, jumping minnows. I gave the minnows to the neighbor for his trouble and used their phone to call the local bait shops.

I quickly found a shop owner interested in doing business with me.

"You are a lot closer than Arkansas," he remarked.

The next day, the owner of the bait shop and his helper drove up to our humble home in their tank truck, ready to do business.

He and his helper unfolded a twenty-foot minnow seine and waded into the pond and seined about one-third of the pond in one drag. It was so full of minnows; I had to help them pull the seine out of the water. There were thousands of flopping shiny minnows, known locally as *shiners*.

The three of us started counting them by the handfuls, twelve minnows to each handful, more or less.

We quit for the day at almost two thousand shiners.

"That is all my tank truck can easily keep alive for a week," he said.

The bait shop owner paid me a penny a piece for the minnows, so I made about twenty dollars on that first day.

They explained they would come back once a week to seine another load of shiners. They said I needed to feed the minnows daily so the fish would learn to come to the top at feeding times, like cattle, which made them easier to seine in one drag.

They left a twenty-pound sack of fish food and told me to throw a coffee can full of feed out at five o'clock each evening.

"We will bring you a sack of feed each week."

They, of course, made a healthy profit on the minnows' sales, but they took all the losses, also.

It felt good to have some money in my pocket; it had been a long dry spell. I realized now that I needed to make my own money and future. No one else was going to help me, and I needed to be my own man.

I entered the seventh grade determined to be on that middle school's honor roll. My grades had improved significantly since my little talk with Mrs. Stewart in the fifth grade.

The city library awarded me some type of prize for the student reading the most books during the summer recess.

I was even given several free passes to the annual Fall Choctaw County Fair.

Mother was not interested in going to the fair, so Sister and I went by ourselves; our first visit. We spent the day looking at the exhibits and midway rides, and then I became curious about all the varied breeds of animals shown by exhibitors at the fair.

Many of the farm animals had won colorful grand champion ribbons in their categories. I talked to some of the farm boy exhibitors and learned that the champion prize ribbons for their animals also carried a cash prize, and that on the last day of the fair, cattle buyers would appear and offer them top dollars for their prize animals. The more I heard, the more I wanted to know about this moneymaking process.

I had saved up several hundred dollars from my minnow sales and working odd jobs for neighboring ranchers, so I decided to try my hand at this business of raising and showing prize animals at the county fairs.

I made arrangements with several of the local farm families to buy some of their purebred chicks, rabbits, pigs, and calves.

In the farm animal business, farmers breed the animals to have their newborns arrive in early spring, so they do not have to be fed all winter and possibly die from the winter cold.

By the following spring, I had thirty Rhode Island Red chicks, six white rabbits, four Hampshire piglets, and a young Brown Swiss bull calf. I built the rabbits cages and a pigpen. We had a chicken shed for the chickens and a barn for the bull calf so they could have shelter from the usual spring rainstorms.

My main focus was on the purebred Brown Swiss bull. If all went well, he was my college passport, since a grand champion Brown Swiss bull could be worth thousands of dollars, or at least enough to pay my higher education costs.

I was already looking ahead to the future. The only way to make my way in this world would be my own labors and with my own money; no other sources were available.

I told Mother about my show animal plans, and she seemed puzzled at all the fuss I was making. She was more pleased when I told her the animals that did not become show animals would become meat for our table.

When I told her about my long-term plans for the Swiss Bull and my college funds, her face got red and she said, "Well, we will see about that!" and walked away—not very encouraging.

I made the honor roll each session of that school year and received small blue booklets proclaiming my special standing. I proudly displayed them in the corner of my bedroom.

The rabbits, chickens, and pigs were old enough and ready to show by that fall. All received blue ribbons, and the Rhode Island Reds received grand champion ribbons at the county fair. But no one was interested in buying chickens, rabbits, or pigs. The real money was from show cattle, and my bull needed two more years to mature before I could show him.

The prize money from that fair was enough to buy my school clothes for the year with enough money left over to buy an old, used 12-gauge pump shotgun from a second-hand hardware store. I could now bird hunt in the woods. Butch was an excellent pointer and retriever of quail. Even though he had no formal training, he was a natural.

I entered the eighth grade with determination to maintain my good grades. One day while in study hall, which was held in the school library, I noticed a new book in the biography section, *To Hell and Back*. It certainly had a catchy title. I read with interest about a young Texas farm boy, who had grown up not far from where I lived. His sharecropper father had abandoned his mother and siblings. The oldest boy, Audie Murphy, had to hold the family together and feed and care for them. His prowess with a rifle kept food on their table. When World War II started, he had his sister change his birth certificate by two years so that he could enlist in the army. He was really only sixteen years old. He went on to become the most decorated American soldier of that war and eventually rose to the rank of major.

I immediately realized this was the kind of man I wanted to be, a man who took charge and cared for his family and rose to the rank of an officer in the army.

My destiny was suddenly clear. I was going to enlist in the military and become a career army officer; but I still had to make sure Mother and Sister were able to manage on their own when it was time for me to enlist and leave our home. I felt it was better to keep my long-term plans to myself in view of Mother's constant concern for the men in her life *abandoning* her.

I certainly did not want to incur the wrath that awaited a man who ever abandoned her.

―――

CHAPTER 10
Bad Winter

• • •

MOTHER WAS RESTLESS AGAIN AND increasingly bitter about her relationships with men and life in general.

She lost her part-time weekend lounge job for some reason she did not want to discuss. After several weeks of sitting at home doing nothing, she announced her plan of action.

"We are broke, and we are going to raise chickens!"

"When did we ever have money to buy chickens?" I asked.

Mother looked at me with a gleam in her eyes. "I know a man who works in Muskogee who owes me a favor, and he will supply us with young chickens. The only catch is we have to go to Muskogee and pick up the chickens."

"We do not have a truck. How can we pick up chickens?" I asked.

That issue did not seem to be a problem to Mother, and late one Sunday night, she and I left Sister sleeping and drove our Ford Coupe to Muskogee, Oklahoma, over an hour north of our place. We arrived at midnight at the prearranged abandoned country road on the outskirts of Muskogee. A large flatbed truck, waited for us with its motor running and its load of chickens very upset and noisy. It struck me as a strange place and time to be picking up chickens.

The driver and Mother talked privately for several minutes. She never introduced me to him. Finally, they reached some type of understanding, and Mother commanded us both to load up our old Ford with crates of chickens.

We loaded first our car trunk and then the back seat and then tied stacks of chicken crates on the top of the Ford. We looked quite a sight, not unlike the Ma and Pa Kettle movies I remembered. Finally, when we could load no more crates of screaming pullets, we drove off into the night toward home, avoiding the main highway and staying on dusty country roads.

We made several more trips on late Sunday nights to that same location to pick up crates of chickens. Soon, we had hundreds of white chickens running around our property until they were fully grown. Several months later, when Sister and I came home on the school bus, all those white chickens were gone.

I ran into the house, hollering, "Someone took all our chickens!"

Mother announced, "I sold all the chickens to a meat-processing plant, and we are out of the chicken business."

She further announced she was going to take the money to Tulsa and invest it and would return in a few days.

The next day, Mother drove away, leaving Sister and I to take care of everything and continue our education. She was gone for over two months, only managing to mail us two letters, postmarked Tulsa, Oklahoma. She explained she was staying longer to earn some extra money and would return by Thanksgiving. She arrived home on the first day of December, looking tired and worn and complaining about *some man* who had taken advantage of her and left her penniless, again.

Sister and I had survived those two months eating the commodities given to us by the state and the wild game I brought home from the fields.

Our diet lacked vegetables and fruit, and it began to affect our health as the winter days grew long and cold and the only heat source we had was that wood-burning cook stove in Mother's bedroom.

Sister missed school due to colds and fever, but I kept going to school each day, even when sick, not wanting to fall behind on my class assignments. I had a constant cough and fever that persisted for weeks.

I struggled to stay in school until the two-week Christmas recess. On the last day of school before the Christmas break, I was so sick from chills and fever, I knew I should have stayed home, but there was a final exam in English that would determine my final grade in that class, and I was not going to miss that test if it killed me, which it almost did.

I barely had enough endurance to finish the exam and stumble to the school bus pickup point. The bus driver stated, "Bobby, you look really sick. Go to a doctor when you get home."

When I arrived home an hour later, I quickly fed the farm animals and went to bed, still coughing and with a high fever. We had no medicine in the house, and Mother said I just had a bad cold and needed to "sleep it off."

I awoke with a jolt in the early morning darkness, a loud noise banging in my head. My body and bed were soaked in sweat, but the room was as cold as a freezer. I was shaking violently. My lungs did not seem to want to cooperate in my breathing. When I coughed, the room started spinning, and I got light-headed. I could not catch my breath, and whenever I took a deep breath, a strange rattling noise came from my chest.

I was suddenly scared, very scared that I was dying. I tried standing up, but the room spun like a top, so I wrapped myself in my old army blanket and crawled on my hands and knees into Mother and Sister's bedroom, where we kept the only source of heat.

The wood-burning stove was cold to the touch, indicating the firewood was all burned. I called out and woke them up.

"What is the problem?"

I saw Mother's shadow rise up from the bed wrapped in blankets.

"I think I am dying, I can't breathe, and I am so dizzy I cannot stand up," I explained in a weak, trembling voice.

Mother threw me a pillow and said, "Curl up behind the stove and get warm and go back to sleep. You just have a cold."

She turned over and went back to sleep. I pulled open the iron door on the stove and felt for the wire basket of scrap lumber we used as kindling and small pieces of firewood and made a fire in the cast iron stove. The room and house were so cold; the fire seemed to have no effect.

I curled up on the cold floor next to the warming stove and passed out, not really caring if my body or blanket was too close to the stove.

The noise of people talking and doors closing woke me later in the morning. It was noontime, and Sister was standing over me with a bowl of chicken soup.

"Mother said to eat this, and you will be fine."

Sister was looking down at me with alarm in her face, recognizing that my normal sleeping place was not on their bedroom floor by the stove.

"Are you okay?" she asked a little sheepishly, not wanting to show too much concern; she had heard Mother say several times I simply had a cold.

"Tell Mother to come here. I need help," I begged, my voice cracking.

Sister quickly found Mother and returned with her in tow.

"What is it, Bobby? I am going to town. Do you want me to get you some aspirin?" she asked.

"No, I want you to take me to the doctor or a hospital. I am very sick," I pleaded.

"You just stay there by the stove. I will get you some more blankets and pillows. You will be okay. You have a bad cold," she explained and handed me another army blanket and pillow.

"But, Mother, I am really sick. I can't breathe, and my chest hurts and my head is spinning, and I cannot even walk I am so dizzy."

"We cannot afford for you to go to a doctor, so just eat your chicken soup and stay warm." She walked away.

Christmas came and went with me lying behind the wood stove, sweating one minute and freezing the next. We never did anything special for Christmas anyway: no presents, no dinner, no nothing. It was just another day around our house.

Going to the bathroom could have been a problem since there was not one in the house. But since I was not eating anything but soup occasionally, there was nothing but fluid elimination to worry about, and I could crawl or stumble onto the nearby porch and pee from the edge of the porch and return to my sick bed on the floor behind the stove.

I grew weaker and weaker as the days went by; the coughing continued, and strange stuff came up my throat and out of my mouth.

Even George became alarmed when I failed to meet him in the woods over the Christmas holidays. He finally got so worried that he came to our house and knocked on our door. He had never done that before because his mother told him not to come to our house because of some rumors she had heard about Mother, and she certainly did not want "her men" around our house.

Sister answered the door, and when George walked into the bedroom, he looked at me on the floor and his face turned white.

"What is wrong with you?" he hollered, holding his face with his hands. "You look like a zombie!"

Mother was not home when George came that day. When Sister left the room, George asked me in a low voice if he needed to have his father call an ambulance to come pick me up. I declined, saying weakly that it was probably too late anyway.

And then George gave me the really bad news.

"We are moving back to East Texas," he said slowly, his chin trembling ever so slightly.

"What? No, you can't do that!" I declared. "We will never see each other again."

I begged him not to move away, but he had no choice in the matter.

Tears were streaming down both our faces as he turned and left. Both of us were very embarrassed by our lack of emotional control and our mutual feelings of helplessness.

The next few days became a hazy blur. I woke up at night coughing and gasping for breath. My lungs produced globs of foreign substance not of this world.

Sister remarked that I was talking to people in my sleep and sometimes screaming before I would choke and wake myself up.

My floor bed and its blankets started to emit a really bad odor. And then a miracle happened. On January 1, I awoke and my lungs were clear, and I could breathe again. My fever and chills were gone. I was still very weak and had lost many pounds, but I had arisen from the dead. I guess it was not my time.

Even Sister was surprised, staring at me in disbelief. Mother was not surprised by my recovery, saying simply, "See, it was just a bad cold."

It was a near-death experience for me, right up there with being run over by a wagon and team of panicked horses, but it would not be the last such death-defying experience for me.

———

CHAPTER 11
Death of Innocence

• • •

FINALLY WINTER RECEDED, AND SPRING sprung into our world. Bitter cold days and cold drizzle gave way to booming thunderstorms and the usual constant threat of funnel clouds.

We were the only family on our county road who did not have a storm cellar, which was notice to the world that we were *really poor*, because everyone in rural Oklahoma had a storm cellar (or as the old-timers called it, their "root cellar") in which they kept their potatoes, onions, canned foods, and smoked and salted pork throughout the year.

I was growing into manhood, moving toward my fifteenth birthday.

Mother's opinion of me seemed to be slowly changing. Always before, I had been her little man, man of the house, and guardian. But now, I began noticing her staring at me from time to time with a disapproving look.

I would ask her why she was staring at me, and she would simply reply, "You remind me of someone," but she never would tell me *who* that someone was.

Mother had been keeping company with a man whom she had met at one of the borderline lounges. He was a man of means and drove a new Cadillac, which looked a little out of place parked in our driveway. He would watch Sister and me with a smile on his face as we walked around and stared into the rich leather interior of the gleaming machine.

I almost fainted one day when he threw me his car keys and five dollars and said, "Take your sister to the drive-in movie in town, and just don't drive too fast."

My heart was pounding with excitement. I did not even have a driver's license, but most farm boys had been driving cars, trucks, and tractors since they were twelve years old without the benefit of a driver's license, so that was not an issue of concern.

Mother quickly approved, knowing that she and her new boyfriend could have some privacy with us gone. I proudly sat tall in the driver's seat and slowly, at first, drove away, making sure to drive through the areas of town where my schoolmates might see me in this marvelous machine.

Raymond and his Caddy would drive up from Louisiana every other weekend during that spring, and Sister and I looked forward to our movie dates at the local drive-in movie theater. And then, it all stopped as suddenly as it had started. Raymond stopped coming to our house. Mother went into a great depression and stormed around our house, cursing Raymond and men in general. She would sit at the kitchen table for hours, staring at nothing.

I tried to focus on other things, such as training my growing Brown Swiss bull. In order to be considered for grand champion station at the upcoming county and state fairs, I needed to train him to be led around by a rope in a large circle and have him stand in various poses for the judges. The bull was more than half grown now and more than a handful to control. I tried roping him and putting a rope halter over and around his head and face, and he immediately jumped and twisted and tried to escape my control. He was stronger than me, and in a pulling match, he usually won.

I quickly realized I needed to use some leverage to get him under control, so I roped him around the neck and immediately wrapped my end of the rope around a large oak tree that stood near our house.

The oak tree proved to be the solution and more than a match when the pulling contest started. The bull eventually wore himself out and settled down to let me put the rope halter on his head and lead him around in circles.

I worked each day to train the bull because that bull was my financial ticket to college one day. A purebred bull of this type that had won several grand champion state fair ribbons was worth possibly thousands of dollars at his ultimate sale.

One fateful day, I had roped him as usual and immediately tied the rope around the oak tree and waited for the bull to settle down, but then he tried something new: attacking the oak tree with his head. In the process, he managed to get himself hopelessly tangled in the rope. Soon, his front legs and head were so tangled in the rope that his head was jammed into the side of the oak tree and the rope around his neck was choking him seriously. The rope was now very tight around his neck, and his front legs were flying around like baseball bats, and I could not get him untangled or release him.

I immediately realized the life or death situation that was occurring and tried to hold his head so he could breathe and screamed for Mother and Sister to come help. Sister ran out of the front door of the house and saw the situation.

"What can I do?" she hollered.

"Where is Mother? I need her help, quick!" I replied.

"She is sitting the kitchen as usual," Sister shouted back.

"Tell her to bring me a knife to cut the rope. My bull is dying!"

She ran into the house and returned with Mother, who was armed with a large butcher knife.

"Hurry and cut this rope, Mother. My bull is strangling," I screamed.

Mother calmly walked over to where I was holding the bull's head so he could breathe and plunged the knife into the struggling bull's neck, expertly cutting his jugular vein, which produced an immediate gusher of blood that pulsed outward for almost three feet. Within seconds, the bull's eyes rolled back into its head and his entire quivering body crashed to the ground, partly suspended in the ropes.

I jumped back in shock. "What have you done?"

Mother just stood there with a strange look in her eyes. Sister covered her face with her hands, whimpered and ran into the house, not to return.

Mother said nothing, looked up at the oak tree, fixed her sight on the lower limb, and said in a matter-of-fact tone, "We need to clean and skin him fast before his meat spoils. Let's get him strung up to that limb quickly."

I stood there in shock and amazement, wondering if this could all be a bad dream.

"Why did you do that?" I screamed!

"Don't give me a bad time, and do what I tell you," she replied with a look in her eyes that I knew better than question. She still held the bloody knife in her hand.

Mother removed the pulley and chain from our water well and backed the Ford coupe under the lowest strong limb of the oak tree.

She climbed on top of the vehicle and tied the pulley to the oak's lower limb, took one end of the steel chain and tied it to the hind legs of the dead bull. She ran the other end of the chain over the pulley head and attached that end to the rear fender of the Ford and slowly drove the car forward as the chain pulled the dead bull off the ground and into the air.

Once the bull was totally clear of the ground, Mother walked back to the hanging animal, plunged the knife into its lower belly, and cut upward toward the bull's chest until all the animal's insides fell on the ground in a smelly pile of steaming guts. She then expertly sliced out the dead bull's liver, heart, and other organs. I could tell that this was not Mother's first rodeo; she knew exactly what she was doing.

Mother then slit open the bull's hide, starting with the hind legs, until a cut had been made in both hind legs from the ankles to its tail. She proceeded to pull the still warm hide down the legs until the leg hide had been removed from the hind legs and was hanging from the top of the bull's butt.

Then, using all her weight and strength, she proceeded to pull that hide down the animal's back and front legs until the bull was just a naked, skinned carcass. In less than thirty minutes, Mother had single-handedly field-dressed and skinned a seven-hundred and fifty pound bull all by herself.

Mother then instructed me to get a handsaw and cut down the center of the backbone of the animal from the butt to neck until the animal was in two large halves.

Mother placed an old bed sheet under the hanging carcass, and with her bloody knife and my saw, we cut the two pieces into two quarters. Two hind and two fore quarters fell into the sheet. When we were done, my college tuition hopes were done, too.

Strangely enough, not a word about this incident passed between the two of us. I saw an awesome example of what Mother was capable of when she was angry and out of control, and I decided it was best to let sleeping dogs lie, so to speak.

The fact that she showed no emotion and worked with the skill of a trained butcher in a slaughterhouse gave me shivers. I often wondered if she really meant to kill my bull or if she was getting back at Raymond for dumping her. In either case, it frightened me that she could explode with such determined killing behavior.

Those images remained with me forever.

———

CHAPTER 12
Goldie and Freddie

• • •

THE HARD WINTER OF '59 gave way to the decade of the sixties. The spring dogwood and redbud trees bloomed. The drab dark woods exploded with colors of white and red, and the brown, dead cow pastures were now ablaze with red Indian Paintbrushes and yellow buttercups.

The sap rose in the pecan and oak trees, and Mother grew restless, again. She announced to us she needed to go back to work at a new *joint*, as rural Oklahoma bars were called, which had opened on the outskirts of town and away from the prying eyes of local state welfare workers.

"They will pay me cash, and I will only work Friday and Saturday nights until about one a.m.," she announced, "and be home by two." And soon began a new parade of men into our home and lives.

Sister and I arrived home each school day night about five-thirty, after our one-hour school bus ride. Mother's day visitors would usually be gone by then, unless someone *special* had caught her attention.

Six years of living in rural Oklahoma had added weight and strength to Mother's body. She was still an attractive woman, having avoided taking up smoking and long periods in the sun.

She was still stocky in build, and could easily lift a bale of hay or sack of feed when necessary. Her facial features were still youthful, with long black hair and dark eyes, which had always attracted men. Some gray hair was starting to show, and her once soft hands were no more.

Sister and I awoke one Sunday morning to discover two new special men in Mother's life, Goldie and Freddie. Mother explained that they were brothers from New Orleans, who were working locally to build a new water system for the town.

Goldie was mother's age, in his late forties. He was a large, redheaded, light-skinned man. Freddie was younger by ten years and dark-skinned with dark hair. He looked and talked like a Cajun, unlike Goldie, who sounded Midwestern. They did not look like brothers to me, and when I pressed them on that issue, they finally admitted they were really half-brothers and laughed.

I immediately suspected they were con men deluxe but kept my thoughts to myself, since Mother was so obviously involved with Goldie and now behaving like a love-struck teenage girl around them.

The two men became fixtures around our house at night and on the weekends. Mother would cook them hearty dinners, and they would often spend the night, sleeping on quilts thrown on the living room furniture or on the floor.

Goldie was a light beer drinker, but Freddie always had a drink in one hand and his bottle of Canadian Club VO in the other. Freddie never had a girlfriend or date and seemed perfectly content to drink himself into oblivion on our couch.

The problems started when Mother announced, "It is not comfortable for Goldie to have to sleep on our floor at night so Goldie and I will spend the nights at a motel room in town, and Freddie will sleep on our living room couch."

Mother had never left Sister and me alone with her male friends before, at least not overnight, and I was uneasy with the situation, and Sister was, too. But there was not much either of us could do about the new sleeping arrangements.

Goldie and Freddie always bragged to anyone who would listen that they were former fighter pilots in the air force. Unknown to them, I was somewhat of an expert in military history and military planes, having read everything I could find in our local town and school libraries about the military.

One night after they had eaten our food at our table and drank several glasses of booze, they started bragging about which of them was the best pilot.

Goldie was not to be outdone by Freddie.

"I could land my P-51 on a rolling aircraft carrier in one pass, and Freddie would have to make several passes before he could summon the courage to grab that cable," Goldie proudly stated.

My ears perked up, knowing that outlandish statement just sealed Goldie and Freddie's credibility issue in my mind.

"I thought you guys were in the air force," I softly asked.

Both men looked at each other, their smiles fading. Then they looked at me. It got very quiet at the table.

Goldie laughed. "We were in the air force, but we were trained to land on aircraft carriers also, in case of an emergency." They waited for my reply.

I sprung my trap, which would seal their fate in my mind.

"Did your P-51s have a rear-seat gunner who operated the tail gun on your fighters?" I asked innocently.

Goldie never hesitated. "Yes, sure did. We called it the *Stinger.*"

Freddie immediately agreed and said, "That's right; it was called a *Stinger*, like a bee stinger!"

They both laughed and changed the subject quickly and never mentioned their flying careers again.

They knew I knew, and they hoped I would leave the matter alone and untold to Mother. They both obviously had never been in the navy or air force and certainly never flew the solely land-based, single-seater army/air force fighter known as the P-51 Mustang.

One Sunday afternoon, after dinner, Mother and Goldie drove away, saying they were going to spend the night at the motel.

Freddie offered Sister and me his extra bottle of VO, but I declined to drink more than one shot in a glass of 7-Up. It was too sweet for me; I preferred an occasional beer of which our refrigerator was now full.

Freddie seemed content to lie on the couch, smoking cigarettes, sipping his glass of VO and 7-Up, and listening to country music on our radio.

Between nine and ten, Sister went to bed. I sat on the back porch, watching the stars and talking to Butch about life in general. He was agreeable as usual and enjoyed the attention.

Freddie walked out the back door, drink and smoke in one hand, and sat down next to me. He was well on his way to becoming totally drunk. He stopped humming "Your Cheating Heart" long enough to ask me if Sister had a boyfriend. A shiver went down my backbone.

I looked into his eyes, and I saw trouble coming. I turned away, mumbling, "No, she does not like boys," hoping that would end that topic. It did not.

Freddie reached in his pocket, pulled out his billfold, and laid a twenty-dollar bill between us on the porch.

"I need about an hour of your sister's time. You want to take my car and go see a movie in town?" he asked, his smile saying one thing, his eyes saying something different. The moment I had been dreading had arrived.

I did not say anything, just got up and went into my bedroom and returned cradling my loaded .22 rifle in my arms. I walked out on the back porch to look into Freddie's alarmed eyes.

"You touch my sister, and I will shoot you dead. Understand?" I left no doubt in my voice.

He hurriedly picked up his money and went back into the living room and lay down on the couch and was soon snoring loudly.

I took Butch into the house, the first time he had ever been in the house, and posted him in the doorway between our two bedrooms, with orders to stay. I then went to bed with rifle beside me. Needless to say, it was a long night.

The next day, Freddie had nothing to say to Sister or me, even when Goldie returned that morning to pick him up. He did not speak to anyone.

Neither of them ever returned to our house after that. Mother never said anything. Finally, after a week went by and Mother had not heard from either of them, she exploded in rage when she came home from town one night.

I was in the kitchen taking a bath in our metal washtub, which sat in the middle of the kitchen floor, near the electric stove where I heated buckets of water to pour into the washtub. I was totally naked, squatting in the tub, which was now too small for my rapidly growing frame.

I could hear Mother talking loudly to Sister about *men* but was not paying attention until all of a sudden the closed kitchen door flew open and Mother came storming in with Sister in tow. Mother pointed at me and screamed, "See, they are all alike."

I stood up, trying to hide my nakedness with my hands. Sister looked away, she being as embarrassed as me and wondering what was going to happen next.

"Take your hands away from your things. I want her to see the only thing men care about is their things." Mother was screaming and pointing.

"Mother, please let me go," Sister meekly pleaded, trying to pull away from her. Mother grew even angrier and grabbed a cast iron frying pan by the handle, raised it over her head, and made a run at me, pulling Sister. I raised both arms and hands to defend myself from that frying pan and was now fully exposed. Sister covered her face with her free hand and tried to look away.

Mother suddenly stopped, laid the frying pan down, and released Sister, who ran from the room. Mother turned and walked away without another word.

I was shaking like a leaf, scared and embarrassed all at the same time. I had come very close to being physically attacked by Mother, and I was at a loss to understand why. I was beginning to fear that in Mother's mind, I was no better than the other men in her life who had wronged her in some way.

Living in the same house with Mother was starting to become more than a little uncomfortable for Sister and me.

———

CHAPTER 13
Repairs

• • •

ENTERING HIGH SCHOOL IS A big event for every teenager. Suddenly, what your new classmates and teachers think of you and your family becomes important. Our modest home was now about the only house on our country road that did not have indoor running water and flush toilets. This was not a big issue for me before high school, but now our living conditions and social status, or lack of it, began to weigh on my mind.

Mother lost interest in our home and its condition after Goldie walked out of her life. She no longer seemed to have any interest in maintaining or improving our living conditions. Each time it rained, we had to use pots and buckets placed in various rooms to catch the water leaking through our decaying roof. Each rain resulted in more leaks in new places. Mother did not seem to consider this a major problem until the leaks started over her bed one night, and then she agreed it needed a remedy.

She announced that one of her lounge customers was a roofer and she would have him repair the roof. Sure enough, several days later, the roofer appeared with his grown son, who was about nineteen, and a load of asphalt roof shingles and roofing nails. In fact, the two men moved into our house, supposedly while they installed the new roof on the house, chicken shed, and outhouse, all of which leaked.

The two roofers ate with us every night for several days and stayed home with Mother during the day while Sister and I were in school. No roofing occurred.

Mother enjoyed the daytime company and made beds on our living room floor for the roofers' sleeping needs at night. They appeared to be in no hurry to do any work.

After a week passed, it became apparent they were perfectly comfortable with their new living arrangements and started to come and go during day and night like they were part of the family. Mother got involved with the older roofer. I did not care much for either of them since they appeared fairly shiftless to me and both smoked cigarettes constantly, and the older man chewed tobacco and always carried a coffee can around to spit in, which impressed me as a pretty nasty situation. I wondered how Mother could kiss a man on the mouth that had tobacco juice stains on his lips.

Mother's standards for her boyfriends seem to be steadily dropping since her breakup with Raymond, and she was no longer concerned about exposing Sister and I to lowbrow characters.

Friday night arrived, and I assumed the roofers would follow Mother when she left for her night job. I was wrong. They stayed at our house to keep Sister and me company. They wanted to play cards and dominos with us and conveniently had bought games recently. The younger roofer flirted with Sister while the older man engaged me in conversation about our farm and our farm animals. Sister was coming of age and enjoyed the attention she was receiving.

After several hours of game playing, the older roofer suggested we play strip poker, and he explained the rules. I felt another of those chills go down my spine. Sister's face grew red, and she suddenly became embarrassed at the thought of disrobing in front of three males. She excused herself and went outside and sat on the porch. The roofers both laughed it off. I announced it was our bedtime.

"Bobby, why don't we all have some fun with your sister?" the young roofer said, and both roofers looked at me to see my reaction.

They had caught me by surprise with their question, and I tried to act casually and not overreact, because I did not want another Freddie situation, which probably had caused Goldie to drop out of Mother's life.

"What kind of fun?" I asked innocently in a normal tone of voice.

"You know!" the younger roofer continued with his approving father looking on with a guilty smile on his face.

"Just ask your sister to take her clothes off and show us her body, that's all. No big deal. Young girls her age like to show off to older guys, don't you know that, silly boy?" he said, trying to make me feel foolish.

"Sister is too shy and has never done anything like that before, so she would not agree to do that," I said, playing for time now and trying to keep the conversation on friendly terms because I did not want a big problem Mother might blame on me; besides, there were two of them.

"Ahhh shucks, Bobby. Don't be such a spoilsport; she would probably enjoy the attention."

"No!" I stood up, announcing with my sudden movements that the conversation was finished.

I walked out to the back porch and told Sister I was uneasy with the two roofers' intentions and told her to go to bed and close and lock her bedroom door. She looked scared, but she got the message and went to bed, and I posted Butch in her bedroom for the night.

I then went to bed, making sure my rifle was within reach. The next morning, everything was as usual around our house. There was tension in the air, but no one spoke of the conversation from the night before.

Before Mother left for her Saturday night work shift, I asked her, "When are those roofers going to finish their work and leave?"

"Next week," she said. "Why, is there a problem?"

"I am concerned about strange men sleeping in our house with Sister here," I said and watched for Mother's reaction to see if she got the message.

"Bobby, those guys would not hurt a flea. What has gotten into you lately?" she replied, her expression and words revealing her growing impatience with me.

I dropped the subject, and she left to go to work without any further conversation.

The older roofer had gone to town earlier that day and brought back two six-packs of Jax Beer, which he had iced down and the two of them now began to enjoy.

They offered me one, which I accepted. As soon as Mother left for work and it had gotten really dark outside, the two roofers asked Sister and me to play a game with them in which one person would look for the other three people with a flashlight in the dark of our backyard and pasture area. There were plenty of places to hide, and it sounded like a fun idea, although more of a child's game than something I would expect from grown men. But everyone was pretty bored at night around our house since we had no TV set. I would have normally just curled up with a book and read until bedtime.

The older roofer volunteered to be it, and the remaining three of us hid the best we could. I found an area of high grass and weeds where I could lay and not be seen but I could watch everyone else's movements. I was still a little uneasy due to the events the night before.

The it roofer ignored Sister and his son's hiding spots and continued to hunt for me until he found me, crowning me with the title of it. I had watched him walk by his son's hiding location and ignore him. This gave me pause.

I played along, and the three of them disappeared into the dark to hide. After the required waiting time, I began my search. I could not find any of them. After a few minutes, I became alarmed. One of the rules of the game was that no one could go into our large barn because it could be dangerous at night in the darkness due to the sharp, pointed tools and equipment stored inside.

Growing more concerned with each passing moment that I could not find anyone, I approached the dark barn and thought I saw the red glow of a cigarette appear in the back doorway of the upstairs hay loft.

"You guys in the loft?" I hollered. "That is against the rules! Get down now before you set the hay on fire."

No reply.

I stuck the flashlight in my back pocket and used both hands to climb the wooden ladder to the second-floor hayloft. I pulled out my flashlight and looked around the loft and could not see anyone. Then, I caught the scent of cigarette smoke and knew someone was hiding there.

I lit the suspected area with my flashlight, and it revealed the older man standing behind Sister and holding her off the floor while his son was pulling off her jeans, which were already down to her ankles. The roofer's left hand was covering Sister's mouth, and she appeared to be paralyzed in fear. Her eyes were wide as a deer's if it was caught in a car's on-coming headlights.

"Let her go, now!" I screamed, grabbing a nearby long-handled hay hook and advancing toward them. They could not see clearly what I had in my hands but assumed the worst, because they released Sister and stood there, more surprised than scared.

"Sister, pull your pants up and get out of here," I ordered. "Go to my room and get my rifle and bring it to me. I am going to shoot some rats!" Now, the roofers looked scared.

Sister hurriedly left the loft, and the three of us stood and looked at each other.

"Bobby, we meant no harm. We were just playing with her, so just relax, and we will leave now quietly and everything will be fine. Okay?" the older roofer pleaded, still not sure what my intentions were. I was not sure either.

Sister quickly returned with my rifle and Butch, who had sensed trouble was brewing. She handed the rifle up to me from below.

"Sister and I are going back to the house and throwing all your stuff on the front porch," I announced. "You need to get your things and leave, and do not come back or you will be very sorry."

They nodded in agreement, and I left them standing there.

They quickly removed their items from the front porch and got into their truck and left. The older roofer hollered toward the house as they drove away: "No hard feelings. Tell your Mother thanks for everything."

I stayed awake until Mother came home that night. I told her the story, and she wilted like a flower.

"Bastards, they are all bastards," she said. "Now, who is going to repair my roof?"

"I will do it. They forgot to take their ladder, so I have everything I need to do the roofing. I will work on it after school each day," I replied, not wanting the roofers to return for any reason.

"You don't know how to roof, and you don't even have a helper," Mother sighed, looking more depressed.

So in the following days, I taught myself how to replace a roof of asphalt shingles. I carried my own supplies up that ladder. It was not easy and took me a week. It was not a perfect job, but we had no more leaking buildings thereafter.

We never heard from the roofers again, and the matter was not discussed again in our home.

I was able to get a weekend job working for a nearby rancher. I helped him cut brush and weeds away from his corrals and buildings and repaired his many miles of barbed wire fencing.

I noticed stacks of galvanized water pipes in his barn. He informed me he had planned to lay water pipes from the county water lines along the county road to his cattle watering tanks in his corrals but had changed his mind and built a windmill to pump water for his cattle.

I asked to buy about fifty feet of his water pipes, and he agreed to let me work it out in trade. He even helped me load it on his truck, and we dropped it off next to our water well. I had plans to bring water into our modest home.

In the next several months, I talked Mother into buying an inexpensive water pump from the nearest Sears Roebuck, and with the help of a plumber who needed one of my pigs for his family's winter meat, we installed the electric pump on our well, buried water pipes into our home, crawled under the house, and brought the piping into our kitchen. At last, we had running water in our house. The job of further indoor plumbing and a hot water heater would have to wait until another day, which never came.

But at least now we had a good roof over our heads and running water in our house.

———

CHAPTER 14

Appeasement

• • •

MOTHER AGAIN LOST HER NIGHTTIME weekend job: "Because a co-worker was out to get me fired, the sorry bitch." At least, that was Mother's story.

She stayed home for weeks in a depressed, weed pulling state of mind. She spent the daylight hours around the outside of our house, hand pulling weeds until her hands were completely green with stains. At night, she held counsel at the supper table and told Sister and me, "I am tired of everyone talking about me and causing our lives to be miserable."

After several weeks of self-pity, she announced one night, "Do not go to the downtown movie house, the drive-in theater, or the county fair anymore. They are not going to get another nickel of our money."

Sister and I looked at each other wide-eyed. Mother had just blacklisted the only three places of entertainment within thirty miles of our house.

"Why can't we go to any of those places, Mother? Those people don't even know who we are," I asked, pleading.

"Because I said so, and I better never catch either of you slipping around behind my back."

Mother looked like she was ready to fight, so I did not question her further. I had recently seen her try to fight a two-hundred and fifty pound man twice her size over a few dollars and did not want to push my luck with her.

I had obtained a short-lived paper route in town to try to earn some money. I felt bad about not being able to continue the route, but the long route delayed me getting home after school until after nightfall, and Mother was screaming at me for being late in feeding our livestock. The newspaper manager still owed me about ten dollars, but I told him to keep it because he had to deliver my route until he could find a replacement and I felt guilty for letting him down.

A few days later, Mother asked me where the ten dollars was, and I told her what had happened. She exploded like a bomb, ordering me to drive her to the manager's house at ten o'clock at night. When we arrived, Mother knocked on the darkened house door until the manager's wife came to the door, a look of displeasure on her face.

"Dwight is sick and in bed," the woman replied to Mother's demand to speak to her husband.

Mother pushed open the front door and walked by the startled woman and directly into their bedroom. I watched as she stormed up to the half-awake but shocked man trying to pull himself up in his bed.

"Give me that ten dollars, or I will beat the hell out of you," she shouted, her voice cracking as she looked around the room for a weapon.

"Lady, Bobby has to sign a release before I can give the money to you, and my records are not here." His eyes and mouth were now open. He was quite frightened at what appeared to be a no-win situation for him.

His wife came running into the room, pulling ten dollars out of her purse and handing it to Mother, who grabbed it and then turned to the manager and said, "Your wife just saved your life, you sorry bastard."

We left as quickly as we arrived.

I was shaking worse than the manager as we drove away. Mother's grim expression never changed, and she stared straight ahead. I had heard stories from others of my mother's outbursts and threats of violence and knew she was not a person to be trifled with when mad. She was very stout and had shown me in the past her skill with killing tools.

Mother kept Sister and me isolated from the general public, for whatever reason I would never understand.

Sister was growing more withdrawn as she grew into womanhood. She had no school friends she spoke about, and she did just enough schoolwork in class to make passing grades. She used no makeup of any kind and did nothing to attract boys' attention even though she was an attractive brown-eyed brunette.

Sister avoided confrontation with others, especially Mother, and followed Mother's directives to the letter.

She seemed perfectly content to play with our younger farm animals and bucket-feed our young, motherless calves.

Occasionally in the summertime, Sister would go swimming in our farm pond as long as I agreed to stand guard and watch out for snakes.

Sister spent more time with Mother than I did because Mother enjoyed having someone to talk to who would listen to her many tales of woe and mistreatment by men. I was now older and I was growing into manhood myself, and I ceased enjoying the often-repeated stories of *sorry men* in Mother's life since she seemed to hate all men in general.

Sister would quietly agree with Mother's assessments and assure her she would never leave Mother's side for some sorry-assed man. Mother always kept her greatest vitriol for our father, "the sorry bastard who abandoned me to raise two children on my own."

One lazy humid summer day between my sophomore and junior year in school, Sister and I were playing Monopoly on the kitchen table. Mother had taken our old crippled Ford Coupe into town to see if she could exchange it at a car dealer for a more dependable car since the old relic was steadily dying of vapor-lock disease.

Sister was uncharacteristically talking loudly about how Mother was driving her crazy, constantly talking about our sorry father and all the sorry bastards in her life. Sister wanted to go to a movie or do anything to get out of the house so she would not have to spend another evening listening to Mother's non-stop harangue about men abandoning her.

I interjected a few words in defense of Mother's depression. "Mother is just lonely. Every man she dates seems to eat her cooking and use her and then dumps her after a few months. I am sure she will get over it as soon as she finds a new boyfriend," I suggested.

Sister stared at me and rolled her eyes. "Bobby, you live in a dream world. Do you have any idea what Mother says about you when you are not here?"

I felt a chill go down my spine. I was not sure I wanted to hear what came out of Sister's mouth next.

"She says you are just like our father! You look like him, talk like him, act like him, and will probably walk out on her one day, too!"

I was too shocked to say anything. I had never really thought Mother considered me in the same league with my father, a man she truly despised. I felt suddenly sick to my stomach, as if someone had fed me poison. I am sure my face must have turned either red or white, because Sister saw my immediate change of expression.

"Please do not tell Mother I told you that. She will kill me," Sister pleaded; now wishing she had kept Mother's secrets.

I weakly said, "Don't worry. I will not say anything to her. She probably would kill you."

I lost interest in the board game and went outside to get some fresh air. I suddenly knew that all the rules of my life had changed and I was correct all along when I felt personally attacked when Mother started talking about all the sorry men in her life. In her mind, I was also one of those sorry men who always used her and abandoned her.

I was confused and hurting, and a little frightened all at once. I had always tried so very much to help my mother with everything that life had thrown our way. I tried to make her proud of me by protecting her and Sister and showing her my school honor roll certificates and other awards that I had earned over the years.

A slow, sickening realization took hold of me, and I knew that one day I too would leave Mother to make my own life, and I felt a shiver throughout my body, wondering how Mother would react the day I left home. I wondered if Mother would simply look away and say with disgust under her breath, "Another SOB gone," or would she react with sudden violence like she did when my poor bull misbehaved? I wondered if her sudden violent killing of my animal without cause was her subconscious way of handling her suppressed anger toward men, and possibly me.

I would be more careful in the future to avoid confrontations with her and try to keep her happy and convinced that I was not just another man who had done her wrong.

—

CHAPTER 15

Heritage

• • •

BEFORE WE MOVED TO OKLAHOMA, Mother would talk for hours about her childhood there as we crisscrossed America in Bill's '49 Ford. She spoke of the backbreaking methods of picking and chopping cotton and how her family would raise and butcher their own farm animals in order to survive and have some food to eat.

She talked about cowboys and Indians, mostly Cherokees and Choctaw Indians, who she grew up knowing. But strangely, once we moved to Oklahoma, she was no longer interested in discussing her childhood or any relatives whom might still live near our new home. I had remembered two small towns in particular from our previous discussions because of their peculiar names, Antlers and Soper, Oklahoma. Why I remembered those towns, I will never know; I just did. They stuck in my mind over the years.

After entering high school, I became aware that two of the towns our football team played against were Antlers and Soper, Oklahoma. Since I discovered that Antlers and Soper were only about twenty-five miles from where we lived, I excitedly asked Mother why we never went to either town to visit her relatives.

"They moved away a long time ago. I do not know where they are or even if they are alive or dead," was her short reply. She showed no interest in further discussing her family's whereabouts, living or dead.

As Sister and I got older, we realized our family was different from other families. We seemed to have no relatives: no grandparents, no aunts or uncles, no nieces or nephews, no cousins, no nothing—just the three of us.

Mother had said our worthless father's parents lived in Minnesota, which was "too cold a place for anyone to live." She insisted she had never been to Minnesota to meet any of our father's family. But Mother slipped one evening when we were having a winter blizzard of blowing snow and freezing temperatures and we were all crowded around that useless wood stove we relied on for heat. Mother said suddenly, "This weather reminds me of International Falls, Minnesota, the coldest damn place on earth."

I looked at Mother, and she looked at me, and we both realized the significance of her statement. Mother looked away, and nothing else was said about Minnesota.

As far as I knew, Mother never made any effort to contact our father or advise him of our whereabouts.

I went to high school with several students who were Cherokee and Choctaw Indians. They mentioned in class one day that their tribes keep records of the names and addresses of all their tribe members.

I could not wait to get home and share this newfound information with Mother, because now she could locate her Cherokee chief father she had spoken of so many times in the past.

When I told Mother the news that night, she seemed more angry than pleased and told us she had no interest in tracking down her long-lost relatives, whether Cherokee or not. I began to wonder about both sides of my heritage, since they did not seem to exist.

More questions arose when it was time to obtain my Oklahoma driver's license when I turned sixteen years of age. That summer I had sold two half-grown heifers to raise the money to buy my first vehicle, a 1953 Ford pickup. It had many miles on it, and being an old pickup, it had no air-conditioner or power extras on it, just a V-8 motor and standard manual transmission. I located a repair manual at a local auto parts store and proceeded to make repairs and bring my old pickup back from the near dead.

I replaced the points and plugs, the brake cylinder, and the electrical system, and worked on the motor, transmission, and carburetor until the old Ford ran like a Singer sewing machine.

When September arrived and I applied for my driver's license, they requested to see my birth certificate. I had never seen it myself. When I asked Mother for a copy of my birth certificate to take back to the license office, she replied it had been lost in our many moves. Mother used some old school records and convinced the license clerk of my date of birth. I received my driver's license and then used it to obtain my Social Security card.

I later grew concerned that I did not have a copy of my birth certificate and asked Mother to see Sister's certificate.

"It was lost, also," she said. "You don't need one anyway; you can always just use your driver's license and Social Security card, which is what I always did."

I dropped the subject but felt uneasy about why this was another off-limits subject in our household.

Now with my junior year of high school approaching, I needed a steady job to be able to buy decent clothes and have some spending money.

There were not many jobs for teenagers my age around our town. In fact, there were not many jobs for anybody who was willing to work.

I learned of a work-study program at Hugo High School called Distributive Occupations, which allowed a student to work and go to school at the same time. Classes would be from eight in the morning until noon, and then the student went to his or her work site from one o'clock until its closing time.

I talked to Mr. Ray Kelly, the director of the DO program, and he informed me all the jobs were taken except for working in the meat department at the local grocery store. He advised me to talk to the owner, Mr. Rob Ford, about that opening. I recognized Mr. Ford's name because my mother did not like him and refused to shop in his grocery store. It seemed she had *words* with him several years ago about her unpaid grocery charge account.

I had never met Mr. Ford and could only hope that he did not ask me who my Mother was. He didn't, and I got the job, making my first hourly wage of thirty-three cents per hour. I worked each weekday afternoon from one o'clock to six o'clock, and then each Saturday from seven in the morning until nine at night, with one thirty-minute break for lunch about three o'clock. I also learned the trade skill of a meat-cutter, which would hopefully lead to better pay down the road.

The meat department manager was a hard worker and an equally hard taskmaster and expected a good day's work out of his staff. I quickly learned that the new boy was expected to do the entire daily clean up of the meat department, which included all the processing equipment, which must be done expertly each afternoon.

All the power saws, grinders, slicers, and meat-handling equipment, even the wood chopping blocks, had to be cleaned thoroughly each night and then washed and sanitized. If it was not done correctly the first time, then it had to be redone until it was spotless. I quickly learned to do everything right the first time.

The new boy also had the responsibility of grinding all the ground meats needed for the entire next day. I started seeing hamburger and sausage meat in my dreams. Needless to say, every tool and piece of machinery in a meat department has been made for the sole purpose of cutting, slicing, or grinding meat and bone, and it doesn't matter to the machine whether that meat is dead or alive. Therefore, a careless moment of daydreaming or lack of attention can leave a worker minus fingers or other body parts very quickly. *Safety* is the gospel in a meat market. You learn hand-eye coordination and learn to be sure-footed when carrying a hundred pound quarter of beef or seventy-five pound crate of leaking chickens because you really do not want to end up on the floor under that object.

The work was hard, dangerous, and sometimes exhausting, and always wet and bloody, but at least I was learning a trade and was earning a paycheck each week.

In the meantime, I was able to keep my school grades and honor roll status and was looking forward to graduation and a future military career.

Things were looking up in my life.

———

CHAPTER 16

Moving On

• • •

By the end of my junior year in high school, life looked brighter to me. I received a raise at my job, now making a whopping forty cents an hour. And with working six full days a week during the summer months, I managed to save enough money to purchase a used semi-automatic .22 Mossberg rifle and a used TV set with roof antennae. Now Sister and I could try to watch TV shows at night, although our reception was poor due to the long distances to the nearest TV transmitter. Mother did not like to watch TV shows. She said they were a waste of her time; she would rather think and worry.

I was doing well in school and enjoyed my classes and teachers. I was meeting new people at the grocery store and enjoying flirting with shopping schoolgirls who came with their mothers, especially one particular brunette from another town.

But things were not going well at home. Mother became more depressed and hostile to just about everything in her daily life and anyone she had contact with, including Sister and me.

She resented the fact that I was no longer dependent on her for any financial support and ignored the fact that I was now able to purchase her and Sister some nice perfume sets for Christmas that year. She ignored that Christmas as she had always done, buying no gifts, and told me that since I worked in the local grocery store and got a ten percent discount on grocery items I could just buy all our needed groceries in the future, which I did, without complaint.

After all, that meant I really was the man of the house now, bringing home the bacon and beans.

Mother repeatedly voiced her concern about her ability to survive after Sister and I both reached the age of eighteen, because her state child welfare check and precious commodities would cease at that point. Her part-time waitress income continued to drop, probably because of her inability to get along with her employers and co-workers. That was becoming an increasing problem. As she often described them, "the sorry bastards" or "sorry bitches" were out to make her life miserable. I assured her I would make sure she had enough food money to get by and not to worry about it.

Mother's love life also deteriorated and she was now dating men whom she would never have considered dating before. Most men avoided Mother because of her increasingly negative and hostile personality. That, in turn, caused her work tips to decrease, adding to her depression.

Mother seldom had anything to say to Sister and me anymore, and our home life reminded me of some of the Edgar Allen Poe stories I had read in English class about *feelings of impending doom* in people's minds.

Mother complained that our neighbors stared at her when she drove by their houses. Her co-workers were also talking behind her back to her employer and to her customers at work.

Mother instructed Sister and me to avoid any social contact with our neighbors or the community at large. She banned all attendance at school ball games and other social activities.

Mother's commands caused Sister to become even more reclusive. Mother even encouraged Sister to skip school and stay home on days of class activities, such as class trips or photos.

Mother had never been the type of mother to hug or kiss us. Sister and I had always been embarrassed when neighbors or our teachers had shown us any affection because it seemed so foreign and uncomfortable to us.

Mother's demeanor took on even more coldness. Her lack of interest in our school grades and social events began to be very noticeable. Finally one night, I could stand it no more, and while she was washing dishes, I pulled up a chair and sat down next to her and said, "We need to talk."

She just looked at me with boredom in her eyes.

"Why are you so cold and angry at Sister and me? We have only tried to love you and help out as much as we can."

Mother made no reply and kept washing dishes.

"You seem to think we have caused all your problems in your life," I continued, my voice starting to crack from the emotion I felt inside.

Finally, Mother slowly turned and avoided my eyes, looking through me, and said, "I really do not feel anything for anyone. I have sacrificed my entire life for you two kids, and I have nothing to show for it. Nothing but pain and poverty."

And with that, she was finished with our conversation and returned to her dishes. She showed no emotion.

I felt a sudden painful awareness that she no longer had feelings for anyone anymore, including us.

For some unknown reason, Mother had detached herself from us and was living in her own world, all by herself. We were now part of the problems in her life, along with everyone else, and nothing we could say or do was going to change her mind.

A realization came over me like a cold chill. I needed to think more about mine and Sister's future needs and not worry so much about Mother, who seemed to be in her own world, a world without much reason or hope for the future.

To add more mystery to her state of mind, she suddenly said she was thinking about moving us and was going to purchase a small house in town in case our house was ever destroyed. She said it was a good investment and someone agreed to help her purchase it for future use. I never questioned Mother about the matter; it made no sense to me. An indoor bathroom in our house would have been a more practical way to spend her money.

This mystery house led to even more confusion in the forthcoming melodrama.

———

CHAPTER 17
A Best-Laid Plan

• • •

By THE SUMMER OF 1962, I was old enough to think about my future career plans. I wanted to become a career army officer. I knew from reading every book and article I could find at the library that I would need a college degree to obtain an officer's rank. I had the grades to get into Oklahoma State University, where I had applied in my junior year, and they had already accepted me. But I did not have the necessary funds. I had saved up only a couple hundred dollars, and that was not enough to become a full-time college student. I had no other source of funding or support.

I discussed my dilemma with one of the grocery store managers where I worked, whom I knew to have a military background himself. He suggested I join the local National Guard unit where he was a staff sergeant. Then I could do my six months of basic training as soon as I graduated from high school and I would also earn extra money and army service time at the Sunday guard meetings before I graduated. Upon completion of my six months army basic training, I could enroll full-time at Oklahoma State University for the spring semester and have the additional income from the National Guard to help pay my college tuition.

This plan seemed to solve my immediate needs, and I signed the necessary National Guard enrollment records on my eighteenth birthday. Now I had a plan and career path to work toward.

Mother had always forbidden Sister and me from dating anyone, and that was never a problem since Sister and I were so bashful and kept isolated from social events. That changed for me in my senior year of high school.

The only social life I had was playing cards or dominos with my grocery store co-workers after work on Saturday nights. Everyone in our store department hurried to clean up and close the store at nine o'clock on Saturday nights, and then we played cards or dominos until midnight. We had firmly established this routine by my final year of high school.

A cute brunette from a neighboring town came into my store every Saturday with her mother. She would linger near the meat department while I waited on her mother's needs. She blinked her brown eyes and smiled at me, and we finally started to talk about our schools and little nothings. Finally, after several weeks, I got up the courage to ask her for a date after work on Saturday night. She readily agreed. She told me she could only stay out until midnight, which was music to my ears because of my own situation at home.

I never told Mother I was dating a girl on those Saturday nights. I did not want the sure emotional confrontation that would arise.

Our several dates never really amounted to much. We drove out to the local cemetery or lake and talked, talked, and talked some more. We were both so bashful that neither of us knew how to do any more than give each other a single good night kiss. During the Christmas school break that year, we drifted apart.

When school started again, my love life took a sudden change. A new girl enrolled in my DO class. Judy was a year younger than me but much more worldly. She had moved to our town to live with her grandparents, for reasons that she never made clear.

She took an immediate shine to me for some reason, and we began talking between classes and after school. She worked at the local hospital.

We started to see each other for a couple of hours on Saturday nights after work. Both of us were pretty tired by then since we had each put in a long day. When she kissed me, my entire body came to attention, and she really knew what she was doing and where my nerve endings were.

As the weather warmed, I suggested we secretly meet on Sunday afternoons at a swimming hole in the deep woods, which was a short distance from my home. We could be alone and unseen.

That first spring day at the swimming hole, we never even got wet. She spread a large beach towel over the warm sand and lay down upon it and called me to her open arms. I melted into her hot embrace and hungry lips.

I later explained my career plans to her, and she seemed impressed with my ambition and was encouraging. She planned to enter nursing college after graduation.

We continued to meet on Sunday afternoons at our secret place as our schedules allowed, and we became very close in more ways than one.

As the end of the school term approached, I asked Judy if she would be my girl and wait for me faithfully until I returned from basic training. She swore she would, so I gave her my high school ring to wear around her neck to seal our commitment.

Graduation day came at high school, with its awards ceremony. Graduation took place on a Friday night. Mother did not attend. She was working, and told Sister to stay home, so I attended alone and made excuses for Mother's absence.

I was still on the school honor roll when I graduated, and my DO class instructor named me student of the year.

My new life was about to begin, and I was excited and certainly ready. It seemed like I was about to walk out of a very long and very dark tunnel into the bright sunshine.

But, alas, as I had read in one of Steinbeck's novels, the best-laid plans of mice and men go astray. Events just did not go as I had planned.

I expected my army orders to arrive the week after graduation. Those orders would have directed me to appear in Fort Polk, Louisiana, for six months of army basic training in their hot and humid swamplands.

For some unknown reason, the army orders were delayed. So I continued to work at the grocery store, and the meat department manager asked if I could manage the meat department while he took a much-needed week's vacation. I accepted his request and assumed the duties of meat department manager with a flourish, proud to have been trusted with that responsibility and determined to do a good job. I was now a skilled meat cutter with two years' experience.

Mother knew I planned to go away for six months of army training, but I had not told her about my plans for Oklahoma State University or anything about my girlfriend. I knew her reactions would be sudden, extreme, and possibly violent, and I just did not want to deal with those issues. I hoped my reassurances of my continued financial and personal support of her and Sister would be enough to keep her from doing something drastic.

It turned out that I was wrong, very wrong.

———

CHAPTER 18
Explosion

• • •

WEDNESDAY, JUNE 18, 1963, WAS a routine summer day for me. Up by dawn, feed and water the necessary livestock; shave and clean up, and out the door to the grocery store to manage the meat department. I arrived at work before seven o'clock. Mother and Sister were still in bed asleep when I left home.

I was four days away from leaving for army basic, and I was eager for the week to end. I hurried home that day, wanting to try out a new fishing lure I had purchased. The summer days were long, and that allowed me an hour or so to fish in our farm pond after work.

Mother was not home when I arrived; she now worked part-time at night for a café in town until about ten o'clock. The café had required her to install a telephone as a requirement of employment at our house, so they could phone her if they needed her on her days off.

I quickly changed clothes, grabbed my fishing rod and my rifle, and headed for the nearby farm pond with an excited Butch running far ahead. I could see Sister near our barn feeding our newborn calves. I waved to her with my fishing rod to signal where Butch and I were headed. She waved back and continued with her chores.

I fished until dark with the Hawaiian Wiggler, and it worked quite well. I caught five bass, keeping the two large ones and releasing the smaller ones.

Butch and I walked back to the house, he now exhausted from chasing rabbits. I cleaned the two bass on the back porch and talked to Sister about the additional chores she would need to do once I left for army training the following week. She was concerned about doing chores that required heaving lifting, such as moving one-hundred pound sacks of feed and seventy-five pound bales of hay.

"Mother is strong as a bull," I assured her, "So it should not be a problem."

I wrapped the bass in freezer paper and stuffed them into our already fish-filled freezer. I prepared and ate a peanut butter sandwich for dinner, went into my bedroom, read a Frank Yerby novel until about ten-thirty, and then went to sleep. Mother had not returned home by then, but that was not unusual; sometimes she stayed out until the early morning hours on the nights she worked.

Sister had already gone to bed, and her bedroom was dark. I immediately fell asleep and was not awakened until, in the early morning hours, my bed suddenly started shaking violently. Someone was screaming at me, "Get up!"

I was very groggy and startled by the sudden awakening and noise. Then the single 100-watt light bulb in my bedroom ceiling blazed on, totally blinding me. I sat up in bed, and the next thing my eyes focused on was the business end of a rifle barrel only a few inches from my face. It was my fully loaded Mossberg semi-automatic .22 caliber rifle with Mother on the other end.

"Get out of that bed, you sorry bastard," she screamed, her eyes wild and red, both her hands violently shaking with a death grip on the rifle.

I instinctively knew I needed to get that rifle barrel away from me and felt a sudden dizziness and wave of nausea sweep through my stomach. Mother had lost her mind, and I was going to die!

My next sensation was wetness on my face and my bare back burning. Someone was shaking me and hollering, "Bobby, are you all right?"

Butch was barking like crazy and trying to lick my face. Every dog within a mile was barking. I looked around and could see dawn was breaking and our house was blazing, totally in flames, and so was my pickup parked nearby. It was a surreal scene.

Suddenly with a loud crash, our brick chimney collapsed onto the top of the burning house, causing the entire structure to become a roaring fire pit.

The neighbor helped me to my feet, and I leaned on a fence post for support. I was shaking badly and confused about everything. I was not sure if I was just having a terrible nightmare and I would soon wake up. I don't remember how it happened, but the next thing I knew, I was here.

Fire trucks and ambulances arrived, and I was taken away to the hospital where I was treated for smoke inhalation, cuts, and burns on my face and back. The doctor told the deputy sheriff that I was in shock and very confused. The deputy offered to drive me back home, and he questioned me about what happened.

I told him I really did not know what had happened. He told me matter-of-factly that my mother and sister were dead and their bodies had been removed from the fire debris and were being taken to Oklahoma City for autopsies. He watched me closely for a reaction. There was none. The deputy could have just as well told me it was Thursday morning, June 19, 1963, and my response would have been the same: nothing. I was totally numb and confused. One thing I did remember that would bother me for years was a very strange odor in my nostrils that I could not identify, and my clothes still reeked of that unknown odor.

The deputy dropped me off at what was left of our house, which was just a big pile of smoking ashes. Another deputy was poking through the ashes to see if anything caught his attention; nothing did. The deputies drove away, leaving Butch and I standing there alone.

Luckily, Mother had not parked her 1959 Ford four-door sedan near the house whenever she had come home, and it was not damaged. My pickup was a smoking pile of metal.

I walked around the outskirts of the house, looking for my billfold, which I had discovered was not in my jean's back pocket at the hospital. I found it in the high grass near where I had been found. Lying nearby was one of my .22 rifles. Its rear stock was broken and each end of the rifle dangled from its leather shoulder strap. I walked over to Mother's car and got the key out of the ignition and opened the trunk. It was full of my clothes and an old suitcase. I stared at the items, trying to understand how they got there. The last time I had seen them they were in our house in our only closet. I threw the broken rifle into the trunk.

One of the neighbors drove up and invited me to stay with them until I could get resettled. I accepted his offer but told him I needed to take my clothes into town and store them and would meet him at his home later that evening. He looked at me strangely but did not say anything.

I drove into town in Mother's car and went to the small house and storage building that Mother was buying across the street from her job site and asked the two renters who lived there if I could store my clothes in their storage building. They looked at each other strangely and helped me carry my clothes and the suitcase into the storage building. They locked the building, and I drove back toward our farm. I found out later they immediately called the Sheriff to report my strange behavior.

I realized at that point that it made no sense to be carrying around a broken rifle in the trunk of the car, and wondered if the two renters had noticed it in the car truck when they helped me unload my clothes. I stopped the car alongside the dirt road to my home tossed the broken rifle into a ditch beside the road. I then drove to the home of the kind neighbors that had offered me shelter for the night.

I vaguely remember the neighbors trying to talk to me that night, but I could not carry on a conversation because

I was still numb and my mind was in total shutdown mode. They finally gave up trying to talk to me and sent me to bed.

The next day, I felt like I needed to do something but did not know what to do or where to go. So I went back out to the burned-out home and fed and watered Butch. He seemed as lost as me, in a daze.

While I was there, three men I had never seen before drove up and introduced themselves as special agents and showed me their impressive ID badges. They said they just had a few questions and would be on their way. They asked me what had happened the afternoon of Wednesday, June 18 and the early hours of June 19. I told them I went to bed and woke up lying in the wet grass with burns on my back and face. That was all I could recall.

They looked puzzled and asked me for more details, which I could not provide. They seemed satisfied and drove away.

My high school Distributive Occupations teacher, Mr. Kelly, drove up then and expressed his condolences and asked me to join his family in town that night for supper, which I accepted.

I hated to leave Butch there by himself, but I didn't know what to do with him. His face was coated with black soot from all the burned debris lying around. I am sure he was trying to understand what had occurred. I realized that no one had fed or watered any of our farm animals, but that did not seem to be important anymore. I was in a dream state, and I was sure I would soon wake up from this nightmare.

I ate dinner with my good-hearted teacher and his family. It was awkward since I could not carry on a conversation or make any sense out of anything that was said at the table. I felt guilty for not shedding any tears or expressing anguish at the loss of Mother and Sister. Actually, I felt nothing: no pain, no loss, no emotion, just total numbness. My psyche had totally shut down, along with my brain.

After an hour of mindless chatter, I excused myself, telling the family I needed to go feed and water the farm animals. When I walked out the front door of their home, I noticed that the rear driver's-side tire on the '59 Ford was flat. That seemed strange, because it was fine earlier. I opened the trunk and took out the jack and spare tire, removed the flat tire, and noticed no nail or other object in the tire. I was throwing it in the trunk when I noticed a familiar vehicle parked a short distance behind me. Three men sat in the sedan, watching me. When they saw me looking at them, they got out of their vehicle and walked over. I recognized all three of them as the special agents from earlier that day.

They said they had some of my property at the county courthouse and wanted me to follow their vehicle to the courthouse. I agreed, and I followed them to the old three-story stone courthouse. It was now dark, and the courthouse was totally empty, except for the sheriff's office, which was on the first floor and was the only entrance remaining open at night.

We walked through the courthouse and up three flights of stairs to the county attorney's office, which was still open and fully lit. I was beckoned into a large, empty conference room, and the three of us sat around the conference table.

The smiles left their faces, and the atmosphere suddenly took on a hostile feeling.

Again, they reminded me they were special agents investigating the fire that occurred, and that they were all arson specialists. In fact, one of them, Weldon Carmichael, a tall, well-built man of about forty-five, was a FBI arson specialist. The other two agents, Chester Stringer and Lile Smith, were both State Crime Bureau arson specialists.

I was suitably impressed; I had never even talked to a policeman before, much less such distinguished special agents such as these.

Lile Smith was the youngest of the three, probably in his early thirties, with dark hair and a short, stout build, and he would have made a good defensive back on a football team. Chester Stringer was the oldest of the three, probably in his early fifties, tall and gray, with a slow drawl like most Oklahoma ranchers in this region; he was a little over weight.

Carmichael was obviously in charge, and the other two followed his lead. That seemed to make sense to me, since he was the federal agent and the other two were only state agents. I would learn months later that Carmichael was not even a law enforcement agent. He was an investigator for a fire insurance underwriter. I would also learn later that this was not the first time that Chester Stringer had allowed a company investigator to pass himself off as an FBI agent during an investigation of a fire. He had been previously sued for such behavior.

Carmichael slapped a paper file down in front of me. "Look at those photos," he said, almost breathing fire from his flared nostrils as he glared at me.

I quickly did as instructed, opening the file cover to look down upon the photos of the charred and blackened corpses of Mother and Sister. I gasped and looked away.

Carmichael continued, "See what you have done."

I looked him in the eye. "I didn't do that! I don't know what happened, but I know I didn't do that!"

Lile now joined in. "We just got the autopsy results back; you shot your mother in the head and then beat your sister to death and then set fire to the house, didn't you?"

"No, I would never do something like that," I said, my voice cracking.

"It's too late for tears now, Bobby. The damage is done." Chester Stringer now joined in. Carmichael was in my face. "You haven't shed a tear since this happened. What kind of animal are you? Why did you have to kill them? Couldn't you just have left if you did not like them anymore?" He was almost screaming now.

"I don't know what happened. I just know I went to bed and woke up in the field. That is all I know," I said firmly, thinking that should clear up any questions and we could wrap things up.

Carmichael's face was now beet red as he slapped down an insurance policy on the table. "We found the life insurance policy and fire policy. That is the reason you killed them, isn't it?"

I looked at the life insurance policy and recognized it was a policy I had purchased recently on *my life*, with Mother named as sole beneficiary. I looked at the small fire policy and noted it was payable to the bank and Mother, not me.

I again looked him square in the eye. "The life insurance is on my life, not my mother. Mother had no life insurance, and I don't know anything about that fire policy. I need to go feed my dog and farm animals," I said and stood up to leave.

All three stood up, Chester and Lile making sure I saw their side arms. "You are under arrest. You are not going anywhere," they all said in unison. I sat down.

I suddenly felt very weak and helpless. I had no one to call to help me, no money, no lawyer and no relatives. I was helpless, and they knew it.

They could do anything they wanted with me, and we all knew it. They proceeded to have their way with me over next four days.

"How did you set the house on fire after you killed them?" Chester snarled. "Gasoline?"

"I did not set the house on fire, and I did not kill anyone," I replied.

"So who shot your mother? Who clubbed your sister? Give us names. Where did you get the gasoline?"

The questions now came endlessly, and all I could say was, "I didn't do anything to anyone or set fire to anyone or anything."

The interrogation went on into the early morning hours. "Still no tears?" Carmichael would say. "Don't you have any remorse or feelings for your family?"

Finally, at about two o'clock in the morning, they called the jailer from the sheriff's office and told him, "Lock him up in solitary and bring him back at nine o'clock in the morning. We have more questions than answers so far, and we can work on him all weekend until we have answers."

The jailer motioned for me to follow him, and I did as told. After all, they said I was under arrest. Of course, there was no arrest warrant for me, but who cared. I was fair game and knew nothing about the criminal justice system, but I was about to learn the hard way.

The jailer walked me out of the courthouse and to the nearby old jail. We walked up the stairs to the second floor and into a hallway of single steel jail cells, each with chipped white paint and a small entrance door. The cells were small with a one single bed frame where a thin mattress would fit snugly against the cell wall. The cell was about four feet wide and ten feet long with one open toilet at the far end, nothing else—nothing to wash in, shave in, or anything else. The jailer slammed the door shut for effect. The noise had the intended result; I jumped and looked into his ugly face. I could tell we were not going to be friends. He knew he was big and ugly and enjoyed his appearance.

There was no one else in this hallway of empty cells, and the jailer turned off the lights as he departed, plunging the area into blackness. So began my days of darkness.

———

CHAPTER 19

Poisoning the Community

• • •

NEEDLESS TO SAY, I DID not sleep in the steel solitary cage where they locked me up. I immediately heard the sounds of scratching little feet on the steel and concrete floors. I had heard that sound before as Butch and I hunted rats in our barn at night. Only this time, I had no flashlight or rifle. I could hear the rats running across the cell floor, but it was too dark to see more than a shadow on the floor. These were not pack rats or small rats; they were large sewer rats with long tails and noses. There were hungry, looking for something to eat—not a pleasant thought. I was afraid to take off my shoes or any of my clothes because I would just be exposing more skin for the rats' inspection. Every now and then I slapped the steel wall of my cell, and the rats scattered. This continued until daylight, when they all disappeared.

At seven o'clock Saturday morning, the jailer arrived and handed me two stale donuts and a paper cup of lukewarm black coffee. He said nothing when I asked him for sugar and cream for my coffee. I soon learned to drink all my coffee black.

He said to follow him to the courthouse, which I did. I was still dressed in the same clothes and had no way to clean up or shave. I ate the donuts and gulped the coffee as we walked up the three flights of stone stairs again to the county attorney's office and the same conference room where the three special agents sat waiting for me.

Carmichael took the lead again.

"This is what we know: you shot your mother in the head and then beat your sister to death. Then you poured gasoline on them and set your house on fire. That is what we know for sure. What we do not know is why you did it and where your missing .22 caliber rifle is. So talk to us and let's get this mess cleared up, and we will let you go to your mother and sister's funeral this afternoon. Otherwise, your ass can sit in jail and rot! So what is it to be, funeral or jail cell?"

I lowered my head and stared at the floor. "I told you last night, I do not know what happened. It is all too blurry for me to remember or understand."

"Where did you get the gasoline? How did you light it?" Stringer asked.

"I did not get any gasoline or light it," I replied, looking him directly in the eye.

"Will you take a lie detector test about that?" Lile joined in.

"Yes," was my immediate reply.

It got very quiet for several minutes. That was the first and last time anyone ever asked me to take a lie detector test. My quick response had rattled them.

Stringer immediately changed the subject. "Bobby, did you have any gasoline around your place? I know farm people always have several gallons of gasoline around their places."

"Yes, we kept two-gallon bottles of gasoline in the corner in my bedroom, since it was the coolest place in the house," I replied.

"Why didn't you keep the gasoline in the barn?" Lile asked.

"Animals would break the bottles, and it might get too hot with all the hay in the barn," I replied.

"Any other flammables in the house?" Carmichael took charge again.

"There were two bottles of kerosene in the attic of the house, over my bedroom. We used it to kill insects and burn brush," I added.

In those days, most farmers and other residents of rural communities, used glass gallon size bottles with screw type lids to store flammables; metal containers would appear in later years and would soon be accepted as safer storage containers for flammables.

Carmichael changed the subject. "Bobby, you had four long guns before the fire. We only pulled three rifles out of the ashes, so where is the other .22 rifle?"

"I will tell you if I can go to Mother and Sister's funeral."

"Deal," they said in unison. "Where is the rifle?"

"I threw it out of my car in a ditch along the road yesterday," I replied.

The three of them looked at each other, and Carmichael continued, "So where was that rifle all along, and where did you hide the clothes you took over to your mother's other house after the fire?"

"I didn't hide anything from anyone; the clothes were in my mother's '59 Ford."

They looked at each other and shook their heads.

"Did you put your clothes in your mother's car before the fire?"

"Not that I remember. Why would I do that that?" I asked.

"Where did you first find that rifle you threw out of that Ford?" Carmichael continued.

"It was lying in the grass near where I was found. I found the rifle when I was looking for my billfold when I returned from the hospital. I threw it in the back of the '59 Ford; *that is* when I first saw my clothes in the car trunk."

"Don't you think it looks pretty bad for you, Bobby? You taking your clothes out of the house before the fire?" Lile asked, probably feeling left out of the interrogations.

"I do not know what started the fire, and I do not know how my clothes got in Mother's car, and I do not know how one of my rifles got in the field," I stated.

"Well, Bobby," Carmichael was now standing over me with his face close to mine. "If you did not kill your mother and sister and set fire to that house, then who did? Anyone else there in that house with the three of you?"

"Not that I know of," I replied. "Only Mother and Sister." I shrugged.

"So you are not telling us that someone else did this, are you?"

Stringer was now also standing over me.

"No, I am just telling you I did not kill anyone or burn that place," I replied.

They were all standing now. "It's noon. We are going to lunch, and you are going back to jail, and then you can show us where the rifle is. We will tell the jailer to let you go with your teacher friend to the funeral." Carmichael was still calling the shots.

They took me back down the three flights of stairs to the jailer, who walked me up to my lonely jail cell and locked me in with a cold plate of boiled pinto beans, which I flushed down the toilet.

An hour later, Mr. Kelly, my teacher, came, and the jailer let me go with him to my mother and sister's funeral. It was all a blur to me. My school friends who attended told the news reporters that I was obviously in a state of shock and spoke to no one and acknowledged no one at the funeral.

Mr. Kelly returned me to the jail and told me that rumors were flying all over town and in the newspapers that I had confessed to killing my mother and sister and burning the house. My heart sunk to its lowest level yet. I was helpless to rebuke such statements and had no one to stand up or speak out for me.

I told Mr. Kelly I had not confessed to anything and it was all just a big mistake. I could tell by his expression that he too was falling victim to all the false information and was wondering how he got involved in this mess.

The three special agents were waiting by their state vehicle when Mr. Kelly dropped me off at the jail. They told me to get into the back seat, and the four of us drove away. I told them to drive toward my old farm. When we had gone about a mile, I told them to pull over to the side of the road, and I got out, walked fifteen feet into the grass beside the dirt road, and reached down and picked up the broken rifle. I walked back and gave it to Carmichael.

They examined it, holding it by its shoulder strap, and asked me how the stock had gotten broken in two.

"I have no idea. That is the way it was when I found it," I answered.

"Looks like you broke it over someone's head to me," Stringer said. "Did you?"

"No, I did not."

We all drove back to the jail, where several newspaper reporters were talking to the county sheriff, Ed Thornton, who was holding court while the reporters were writing. This seemed strange to me since I had never talked to the sheriff myself, only to two of his deputies at the fire scene and the three special agents.

The three agents walked me back up the courthouse stairs to the county attorney's office, and the four of us gathered around the conference table again for more interrogation. I was now in my third day of interrogations by these agents, never having talked to a lawyer, and no one had told me I had the right to remain silent or that anything I said would be used against me. I was easy pickings for them.

I would learn a week later that the sheriff had informed the reporters that I had confessed that my mother was killed with my found rifle, my sister was hit over the head with that rifle, breaking it, and that I had poured gasoline all over the house and lit a match to it. And then I asked for lawyer.

Of course, all these newspaper statements and the sheriff's press releases were completely false, and the agents knew they had to get something concrete before Monday morning because they did not even have an arrest warrant for me yet. They knew that the county judge would have to appoint an attorney for me Monday and everything would be more formal when the county attorney filed criminal complaints against me.

The agents continued to question me into the night Saturday, only breaking for an hour while they all went out to eat and they sent me back to the jail cell to stare at a plate of stewed potatoes, which I also flushed down the toilet. I had no appetite.

We resumed our interrogation room ordeal until eleven o'clock Saturday night. The remainder of the evening was consumed with their same questions over and over, and my same answers over and over.

Finally, they announced that they needed a break, and the three of them walked out of the county attorney's office and loudly walked down three flights of stairs and out the sheriff's entrance to the courthouse. They left me seated at the table by myself and left all the doors behind them standing open. It was obviously a trap to see if I would try to escape. They had been relentless in their interrogations and were getting nowhere in their efforts to wear me down.

They were gone for an hour and returned about midnight and announced they would resume where they left off Sunday morning. They walked me down to the jailer to return me to my cell.

Stringer turned to me and said, "Bobby, you could probably use a bath and change of clothes. Would you like that?"

I agreed heartily, knowing that I was now very ripe and looked like I slept in my clothes, which I had.

Stringer took the jailer aside and spoke with him, and then the jailer motioned me over to the entrance of the jail. The two of us walked up the one-story stairs to the cells.

Instead of taking me to my usual small cell, he motioned me into an enclosed shower area and told me to take off my clothes and get into the shower cell, which had its own cell door.

I took all my clothes off and handed them to him and walked into the shower cell and turned on the wonderful hot water. I heard him close and lock the cell door behind me. I washed my hair with the only bar of soap in the shower and washed my body thoroughly. I rinsed off the soap and turned off the water and yelled, "I'm finished." No reply. I hollered again and beat on the cell door until my hands were swollen. No reply. All the lights were off in the jail, and it was deathly quiet. It now dawned on me, he was not coming back, and I was there for the night in a shower cell, with no mattress, no clothes, no towels, no nothing. Just when I thought I had reached bottom, the bottom fell out, again.

Even though it was the middle of June, I was soon very cold with no way to dry. I was dripping wet from head to toe with nothing to sit or lay on. I propped myself up in a wet corner of the shower stall and shivered the remainder of the early morning hours. I did not sleep.

At eight o'clock, the jailer appeared with a smirk on his ugly face and handed me my same clothes.

"Get dressed. They are waiting for you in the county attorney's office," he ordered.

"I need a towel and something to use to brush my hair down," I pleaded.

He just looked at me and his smirk broadened. "Get dressed, I said!" He handed me two stale donuts and a cup of lukewarm black coffee.

He waited impatiently while I pulled on my dirty clothes, and then we walked out and up those three flights of stairs again to that familiar conference table. The courthouse was very quiet except for the sound of our steps on those stone stairs.

I was told to sit down and wait by the jailer, who said the agents were bringing a *friend* to see me. I could not imagine I even had a friend anymore after what I had been through the last few days, especially after Mr. Kelly told me what the rumors and newspapers were saying about how bad I was.

I had not slept since Thursday night, which was a fitful sleep at best. My total food intake had consisted of stale donuts and weak coffee.

I heard voices coming, and suddenly Judy, my girlfriend was standing there surrounded by the agents. She had been crying, and her eye makeup was streaming down her cheeks. She ran into my arms and started crying, causing me to choke up.

I had not seen or heard from her since Thursday, when we talked briefly at her grandparents' home, and I had assured her I was all right and uninjured. Finally, she looked into my eyes and said, "Bobby, Bobby, what have you done?"

I looked at the agents, and they looked away, not wanting to make eye contact with me.

"Bobby, they said I helped you kill your mother and sister! Tell them it is not true. I never met your mother and sister. Tell them!"

I just looked at the three agents' faces.

"You guys know she had nothing to do with anything. Why are you doing this to her?"

Carmichael took the lead. "Bobby, you tell us what really happened, and we will not charge her and she is free to go. Otherwise, we have to follow the evidence."

The last four days' events and lack of sleep, food, or support had finally taken its toll. I sighed and sat down.

"Okay, let her go and leave her out of this, and I will give a full statement."

I put my head down into my folded arms. I was crashing emotionally and physically, and they knew it. I had lost my will to resist and just wanted some peace and quiet. I just wanted it all over and done with. I was beat and exhausted.

They told Judy she could go. They went to get a tape recorder from the county attorney's office. They even got me a Coke out of the Coke machine, a first. They turned on the recorder, introduced everyone, and told me to tell the truth and nothing but the truth.

I took a deep breath and recited the events of that Wednesday night: coming home from work, fishing, going to bed, and waking up suddenly to find my crazed mother pointing a loaded gun in my face. I remembered thinking I had to get that gun barrel out of my face before she could shoot, and then the next thing I remembered was lying face down in the wet grass with our house on fire and blazing in the background. That was it; they knew the rest of the story—end of statement.

"That's it?" Stringer said.

"Pure bullshit!" Lile reported in.

Carmichael reared back in his chair and announced, "Well, I guess that is that. We can go home now."

It was now about six o'clock Sunday evening. The next day was Monday, and things would begin to get more official and the rules of law would start coming into play, or at least they were supposed to.

All the local and statewide media had been spoon-fed information leading to the obvious conclusion. I had murdered my mother and my sister and burned everything to the ground; there could be no doubt.

There was only one issue that remained unresolved and continued to be a thorn in the side of these special agents. Why? They would work on that puzzle next week.

———

CHAPTER 20
The Final Touches

• • •

THAT FOLLOWING MONDAY DAWNED WITH the jailer bringing me my usual morning breakfast of two stale donuts and a cup of black coffee.

He announced I needed to get ready to go to court in an hour. That took little preparation since I still wore the same clothes and had no way to shave or comb my hair or otherwise prepare for such an event.

The newspapers and media had been busy over the weekend broadcasting to every citizen and potential juror in the State of Oklahoma their version of the facts of my arrest.

The county attorney, Ralph Jenner, who I had not yet even met, had stated to reporters that I would be formally charged with two counts of murder that day. He advised the press that I had admitted to everything: starting the fire, shooting my mother, clubbing my sister to death, and hiding the murder weapon in the deep woods near my house before I had been arrested the previous Friday. He had applauded the county sheriff, Ed Thornton, and the three special agents, Carmichael, Stringer, and Lile, for their great investigative job in solving the double murder so quickly.

He made no mention of a possible motive for the double killing or why a model student and young man would have committed such an act. The wheels of justice started moving slowly that day.

When the county judge sent the word, the jailer hollered my name and we started the walk to and through the courthouse. It was packed. County workers, persons with county business, and many just curious people of the town filled the hallways and stairs to see *the outlaw*.

I was paraded through the courthouse and up those long stairs to the county courtroom. Reporters were already seated. I was wearing dirty clothes and had unwashed and uncombed hair and several days worth of beard stubble. I certainly looked like an outlaw.

Mothers pointed me out to their gawking children and held them tightly in case danger arose.

The county attorney and the county sheriff had been making hand-shaking rounds in the courtroom when I entered. Strangely enough, I had never been put in handcuffs by anyone, nor would I ever be by the investigators or sheriff's officers. It was as if they knew I was not guilty of anything, but they just had to play their respective parts in this melodrama, but I should have no hard feelings since it was not personal.

I had to stand in front of the courtroom, facing the judge's bench. The county attorney did all the talking, and he seemed impressed with all the attention his booming voice attracted.

The county attorney looked familiar, and I stared at him until it dawned on me he looked like the prosecutor in the movie *Inherit the Wind*, with his wide suspenders holding up baggy pants and his overweight frame and loud voice. He had a balding gray head and was near sixty years old.

The county judge was an even older man and a small man just barely visible over his bench. The judge enjoyed the attention, also, which was a change of pace from his usual probate duties.

The judge notified me that I was charged with two counts of murder and would be held without bail. He advised me for the first time of my constitutional rights. He inquired if I had legal counsel or the money to retain counsel. I told him no, and he appointed a local attorney to represent me, a Vester Songer, the former county attorney.

Mr. Songer took me aside and spoke briefly to me and suggested that I should enter no plea at this time but stand moot, whatever that meant. He also said someone would have to be appointed by the court to administer my mother's estate, because I could not, since I was under twenty-one and also charged with killing her. He further told me to give no more statements to law enforcement officials. It was all very confusing to me, and I just agreed to go along for the ride.

I was then taken back to the jail to my solitary steel cell. The jailer brought me a bowl of lukewarm pinto beans and two slices of day old bread. I was so hungry by then that I ate all of it. It had no taste whatsoever: no salt or pepper, no meat, no flavor, no seasoning of any kind.

I started having visitors, which was a first. The jailers had not allowed visitors at all until after the first court appearance.

The manager of the meat department at the grocery store where I worked was one of the first people to come see me. He seemed more embarrassed to be there than anything else. I told him I was sorry his summer vacation got cut short by my family's untimely death.

He told me he understood and then told me the *real reason* he was there. The agents had asked him to question me as to why I had done what I did.

Now I knew why he seemed so uncomfortable talking to me. He had only been allowed to see me so the investigators could gather more evidence against me.

"Bobby," he said, "You and I have always been good friends and hopefully always will be. If you do not want to tell me about what happened at your place that night, it is okay with me."

My voice cracked. He was the only person I trusted, and I did not know what to say to him. I kept it short. "I really do not know what happened or why it happened," I said. "It just did, and I cannot explain it."

Tears welled in my eyes for the first time. Now, we were both embarrassed.

"What can I do for you, Bobby?" he asked.

"Please feed and water my dog, Butch. He will starve to death waiting for me to come home! He is all I have left."

He agreed to help with Butch and shook my hand and left.

A few hours later, the jailer brought the local newspaper publisher, Jack Stamper, to my cell—another visitor, and the second that day. He introduced himself. I had never met him before. He owned the only newspaper in town.

He held out his hand through the bars and stated, "I am a Christian and hold my faith seriously. I want to do what I can to help you. Do you go to church, Bobby?"

"I went when I could," I replied. "I was baptized by the local First Christian Church several years ago."

He changed the subject quickly.

"Bobby, you probably know that many serious and bad things have been said and published about you in the last few days." He kept on talking without taking a breath. "And, now, it's time *you* get to tell your side of what happened last Thursday. I want to print *your version* of the events everyone is talking about."

I felt relieved and encouraged by this man, obviously a man of faith who could be trusted. And he was not a cop, so maybe he really did have my best interests in mind or at least the desire to print my side of this terrible story.

In a rush, I told him the same things that I had said Sunday night to the county attorney's tape recorder. He wrote everything down, thanked me, turned, and left. I felt a wave of relief go through my body. At last, someone was going to print my side of this story in the local paper. There was hope.

An hour later, I was surprised when the editor returned, this time with a printed document in his hand.

"Bobby, I got to thinking about our conversation, and I want to do you right, and I am going to print your signature under your version of this story in my newspaper so the entire community knows you approved it."

He handed me a pen and several typed pages, and I read them eagerly. I immediately recognized this was not what I had told him earlier. I looked at him questioningly.

"This is not what I told you, and I cannot sign this. It is mostly false and not what I told you."

I handed him back the papers. My heart fell through the floor. I knew now why my store manager and the editor had been allowed to see me that day. The agents wanted their version of a full confession that they could never seem to obtain, and they were using others in hope of getting it from me, not taken by a lawman.

"Okay, Bobby." The kindness and empathy were gone from his voice now. He handed me a black marking pencil he happened to have with him.

"Black out what you do not approve and then sign it."

I blacked out most of what was a full confession to a double murder and arson and signed my name to it, all of course without legal counsel. He took the papers and left without another word. I made a big mistake in trusting him, because then his newspaper printed my signature under my supposed confession in the local newspaper the next day. His article asserted my mother and I had differences, and I was sorry we could not settle them in a more peaceful manner. The implications were obvious.

In effect, the agents had obtained a motive for the entire tragic event, something that they could never find previously. Any question in people's minds about what had occurred that morning was now erased by my signature under an article in which I stated I was *sorry* for what I had done.

The die was cast, and my nightmare would now grow in earnest.

MOTHER'S PARENTS: CALLIE & GEORGE WINKLER
AND HER TWO OLDER SISTERS: ARIE & GOLDIE. NOTE: (NELLIE)
MOTHER'S DARK HAIR AND HER TWO SISTERS' BLOND HAIR.

MOTHERS' PARENTS SEPARATED AFTER HER BIRTH AND
SHORTLY AFTER THIS PHOTO WAS TAKEN.

CALLIE RAN OFF WITH THE FAMILY'S SERVANT.

Charge Prepared In Hugo Slayings

By Rob Farquhar
Of the State Staff

JAILED in Hugo in connection with the slaying of his mother and sister, Bobby Wilson, 18, has admitted burning the family farm home and burying a rifle believed used in the slayings. County Attorney Ralph Jenner said he will file charges Monday.

HUGO — The boy everybody described as "ideal" attended the funeral of his mother and sister Saturday, and later was locked in a jail cell to await filing of murder charges which County Attorney Ralph Jenner says will come Monday.

Bobby Wilson, 18, was jailed after leading officers to a heavily - wooded area near his family's home where he said he buried a rifle.

County Sheriff Ed Thornton said Saturday the .22 caliber weapon apparently was the rifle with which Mrs. Lavonne Wilson, 50, was shot and her daughter, Judy, 17, beaten to death.

He Admits Setting Fire

First believed to have died of fire injuries in a blaze that razed their home Thursday, the pair later was discovered to have been murdered.

Jenner said the youth admitted Saturday setting fire to the farm house, 3½ miles north of Hugo.

Young Wilson, who claimed Friday he fled the burning home by jumping through a window, told officers Saturday he set the house ablaze, Jenner said.

'Did You Do It?'

Sheriff Thornton said the following conversation between him and the youth took place in the county attorney's office:

"Was your mother shot with this rifle?" he asked Wilson.

"Yes," was the reply, the Sheriff said.

"Was your sister hit over the head with it?"

"Yes."

"Did you do it?"

"I've already talked more than I should have and my lawyer has advised me not to answer any more questions," the youth was quoted as saying.

Thornton said Wilson lat-

gallon of gasoline all over the house and lit a match to it."

Young Wilson was found by neighbors about 100 yards from the scene. He suffered minor burns. Officers arrested the youth late Friday night and held him for questioning.

Wilson, described by Hugo residents who knew him as a "model young man," told officers who had quizzed him further about the rifle that he was ready to lead them to it Saturday morning.

Rifle to Be Checked

Officers had found the charred barrels of three other weapons in the ruins of the home Friday but the youth had maintained a fourth weapon had been stolen.

"We are sending the gun to Oklahoma City to see if it is capable of being compared with the bullet" that killed Mrs. Wilson, Jenner said.

He said the butt of the weapon was broken off, and "there is a possibility the girl was struck with the butt of a gun."

At the funeral Saturday, young Wilson sat with friends. Ray Kelly, diversified education teacher at Hugo High School, and Cecil Ford, Hugo grocer who had employed the youth part-time.

Observers said the youth appeared to be suffering from shock as Rev. Bill Sikes, pastor of the First Christian Church, conducted

(Continued on Page 2, Column 1)

the services. He was graduated from Hugo High School a short time ago, and was to enter military training Monday.

It was moments after the victims were buried in a single grave at Mount Olivet Cemetery that the Wilson youth told officers he would lead them to the rifle.

Jenner said young Wilson had told officers earlier Saturday he found his mother and sister dead on the floor of the bedroom and that he moved them onto the bed, where the bodies were found Friday.

The youth, Jenner said, gave no reason for burning the home or for hiding the rifle.

Ed Thornton said officers found clothing belonging to young Wilson, personal family papers, including insurance policies, pictures of Mrs. Wilson and Judy and a ring belonging to Mrs. Wilson in a residence owned in Hugo by Mrs. Wilson and in the trunk of the Wilson car.

Publication: The Oklahoman; Date: Jun 24, 1963; Section: Front page; Page: 1

TYPICAL NEWSPAPER ARTICLE PRINTED THROUGHOUT COUNTY AND STATE ABOUT DEATHS.

CERTIFICATE OF DEATH

STATE OF OKLAHOMA · DEPARTMENT OF HEALTH

019821

PLACE OF DEATH		2. USUAL RESIDENCE (Where deceased lived. If institution: Residence before admission)	
a. COUNTY Choctaw		a. STATE Okla.	b. COUNTY Choctaw
b. CITY, TOWN, OR LOCATION Hugo	c. LENGTH OF STAY IN 1b 12 yrs.	c. CITY, TOWN, OR LOCATION Hugo	
d. NAME OF HOSPITAL OR INSTITUTION (If not in hospital, give street address) Residence—		d. STREET ADDRESS	

e. IS PLACE OF DEATH INSIDE CITY LIMITS? YES ☐ NO ☐	e. IS RESIDENCE INSIDE CITY LIMITS? YES ☐ NO ☐	f. IS RESIDENCE ON A FARM? YES ☐ NO ☐

NAME OF DECEASED (Type or print)	First Lavonne	Middle Wilkler	Last Wilson	4. DATE OF DEATH	Month June	Day 20,	Year 1963
5. SEX Female	6. COLOR OR RACE White	7. MARRIED ☐ NEVER MARRIED ☐ WIDOWED ☐ DIVORCED ☐	8. DATE OF BIRTH Nov. 26, 1913	9. AGE (In years last birthday) 49	If UNDER 1 YEAR Months Days	If UNDER 24 HRS. Hours Min.	

10. USUAL OCCUPATION (Give kind of work done during most of working life, even if retired) Waitress	10a. KIND OF BUSINESS OR INDUSTRY Marbut's Cafe	11. BIRTHPLACE (State or foreign country) Unknown	12. CITIZEN OF WHAT COUNTRY? USA

13. FATHER'S NAME Unknown	14. MOTHER'S MAIDEN NAME Unknown

15. WAS DECEASED EVER IN U.S. ARMED FORCES? (Yes, no or unknown) (If yes, give war or dates of service) No	16. SOCIAL SECURITY NO. 566—07—8101	17. INFORMANT Robert Wilson	Address Hugo, Okla.

18. CAUSE OF DEATH [Enter only one cause per line for (a), (b), and (c).]

PART I. DEATH WAS CAUSED BY:		INTERVAL BETWEEN ONSET AND DEATH
IMMEDIATE CAUSE (a) *Dead on arrival*		
Conditions, if any, which gave rise to above cause (a), stating the underlying cause last.	DUE TO (b) *Burns, general, extensive*	
	DUE TO (c) *Gunshot wound of head*	

PART II. OTHER SIGNIFICANT CONDITIONS CONTRIBUTING TO DEATH BUT NOT RELATED TO THE TERMINAL DISEASE CONDITION GIVEN IN PART I(a) *Epi & epidural hemorrhage brain, multiple fracture*

19. WAS AUTOPSY PERFORMED? YES ☑ NO ☐

20a. ACCIDENT ☐ SUICIDE ☐ HOMICIDE ☐	20b. DESCRIBE HOW INJURY OCCURRED. (Enter nature of injury in Part I or Part II of item 18.) *Burned, general, severe, & G.W. head.*

20c. TIME OF INJURY	Hour 4	Month, Day, Year June 20, 63

20d. INJURY OCCURRED WHILE AT WORK ☐ NOT WHILE AT WORK ☑	20e. PLACE OF INJURY (e.g., in or about home, farm, factory, street, office bldg., etc.) Home	20f. CITY, TOWN, OR LOCATION North of Hugo	COUNTY Choctaw	STATE Okla.

21. I attended the deceased from Never , to , and last saw alive on . Death occurred at 5:00 a. m on the date stated above; and to the best of my knowledge, from the causes stated.

22a. SIGNATURE M.D.	22b. ADDRESS Hugo, Okla.	22c. DATE SIGNED 25AUG63

23a. BURIAL, CREMATION, REMOVAL (Specify) BUR-IAL	23b. DATE June 22, 1963	23c. NAME OF CEMETERY OR CREMATORY Mt Olivet	23d. LOCATION (City, town, or county) Hugo	(State) Okla.

DATE REC'D. BY LOCAL REG. 11-20, 1963	25. REGISTRAR'S SIGNATURE Thelma Williams	26. FUNERAL DIRECTOR ADDRESS Coffey Funeral Home, Hugo, Okla.

State Department of Health
State of Oklahoma
OKLAHOMA CITY, OKLAHOMA 73117

I hereby certify the foregoing to be a true and correct copy, original of which is on file in this office. In testimony whereof, I have hereunto subscribed my name and caused the official seal to be affixed, at Oklahoma City, Oklahoma, this date.

July 24, 2001

CERTIFIED COPY MUST BE VALIDATED IN THREE COLORS

John C. Burk
STATE REGISTRAR
OF VITAL STATISTICS

MOTHER'S DEATH CERTIFICATE
CAUSE OF DEATH: "BURNS AND GUNSHOT TO HEAD."
TIME OF DEATH: 5:00 A.M.

MOTHER'S SOCIAL SECURITY APPLICATION DATED MARCH 1937
SHOWING HER ASSUMED NAME OF "LaVONNE WINKLER WILSON
AND BEING
"DIVORCED" AND "BOTH PARENTS DECEASED"
25 YEARS OLD.

Verdict Favors Wilson In Amnesia Case Here

After deliberating a total of 2 hours and 15 minutes, a district court jury returned a verdict in favor of Robert Wiste (Wilson) at 9:45 p.m. Friday.

The verdict's meaning was that, in the jury's opinion, on the basis of evidence present-ed, Wilson had amnesia at the time his mother and sister were killed in June of 1963.

Wilson was charged with murder in the deaths of his mother, Mrs. Yvonne Wilson, and sister, Judy, whose bodies were f o u n d in the charred ruins of the family home north of Hugo.

A jury hearing testimony in the murder charges in March, 1965, was discharged after being reported deadlocked.

The special issue heard this week, one of the first if not the first of its kind to be heard in Choctaw County, was to de-termine if Wilson suffered am-nesia and mental impediment prior to the deaths of his moth-er and sister nearly three years ago. An Oklahoma City psychiatrist, Dr. Moorman Prosser, said that in his opin-ion, based on findings in ex-haustive tests and examina-tions administered to Wilson, that Wilson was unable to re-call events of a certain period prior to the two deaths.

Dr. Prosser, under question-ig by Jack Swidensky, assis-tant attorney general, assist-ing County Attorney Ralph K. Jenner, in the case, said that he does consider Wilson sane at the present time.

NEWSPAPER ARTICLE ABOUT JURY'S FINDING OF BOBBY'S AMNESIA

PHOTO OF BOBBY ON HIS WAY TO WORK TAKEN
SHORTLY BEFORE THE KILLINGS OCCURRED.

COURTESY OF HIS HIGH SCHOOL PAL, JIM MURPHY.

CHAPTER 21
Hard Times

• • •

THE SEWER RATS RETURNED IN growing numbers that night. They ran up and down the length of the floor of the jail cell. They lost their fear of me. They would run under my small bed and sit in the darkness under me, waiting to see if I made any movement. At first, I would yell or slap the steel walls, and they would scatter and run from under my bed. But as the night grew darker and quieter, they grew bolder.

Sometime after midnight, I drifted into sleep, only to be suddenly awakened by something pulling my hair. I jumped up from the bed, and a large rat flew from my head. I suppose he was trying to make a nest or something from my unwashed and matted hair. My hair looked like a mop, so I could understand the rat's confusion.

I realized that falling asleep made me vulnerable to the rats, which were probably as hungry as I was. I drifted back to sleep, and within a few minutes, I was startled by a rat chewing on the top of my head; this time I felt his sharp teeth. I crashed the top of my head into the steel wall hard enough to smash his head, and then I kicked his body until it quit moving. I kept his battered and bloody body on the floor of my cell for his comrades to view and finally got some sleep.

By now, I was familiar with the menu and feeding times in the jail. I was the only person being held in the solitary confinement section of the county jail. There were other prisoners in the jail, but they were caged in what is known as the bullpen, an open area on the opposite side of the jail from where I was located. There was a solid partition steel wall between the part I was caged in and the bullpen section. Breakfast for all the prisoners each morning was two stale donuts each and one cup of lukewarm coffee.

Lunch was a plate of pinto beans, which had been cooked with no meat, no seasoning, and no nothing. It was served with two slices of day old bread.

Supper was a plate of unseasoned, boiled, cut up potatoes and two slices of day old bread. That was the daily menu. It was never to change.

I learned the old county jail was built in 1913, and it looked and smelled like it, rusty and moldy.

Mr. Kelly, my DO high school teacher, was allowed to see me the next day. He informed me that the sheriff had only approved him; Vester Songer, my lawyer; RD, my former store department manager; and my church's preacher to have visitation privileges.

RD was the son of the local justice of the peace, so I am sure that factored into the sheriff's decision-making process.

I asked Mr. Kelly if any of my high school friends could visit me, and he said that was not to be allowed. I had heard several had tried to visit, including Judy, and been denied access.

Mr. Kelly had been appointed temporary administrator of my mother's small estate since he knew my situation and me and was a reputable member of the community. No one else was interested in being involved in this infamous situation.

He also gave me more shocking news. The agents had informed him that they discovered my birth certificate in my mother's records, and my last name was not Wilson; it was Wiste—the same for my sister.

Sister and I had always lived with the last name of Wilson, and so had my mother. Now I knew why Mother did not want to give me my birth certificate or ever discuss the issue.

Mr. Kelly also gave me more surprises; the local authorities had tried to contact my father or other relatives of mine and had found nothing. They also found no record of any previous marriages, divorces, or birth certificates involving my mother. It was as if our family had never existed. He did give me an old envelope with a return address on it to Eureka, California, which apparently was my father's last known address. It was a hotel. His last name of Wiste was listed on Sister's and my birth certificates. No records other than that could be located on either side of the family.

Mr. Kelly said he had to sell Mother's '59 Ford sedan to pay for the funeral expenses. He was going to take charge of Mother's property and try to care for our animals the best he could. He promised to look after Butch for me.

I asked Mr. Kelly how much longer the sheriff planned to keep me locked in this small steel cage, and he said he would try to have the sheriff move me to a larger area of the jail known as the bullpen, which was where the other jailed prisoners were kept.

I told him about the rats and poor food, and he told me to be strong and hopefully things would get better now that the police had all they wanted out of me. That sounded depressing.

Mr. Kelly said my court appointed lawyer told him, "Things do not look good for Bobby. The county attorney has all the proof he needs to make his case in court."

That sounded even grimmer.

"That local newspaper article with your signature on it has been very troubling to everyone, even your long-time friends."

I read his expression and realized that even he was now having misgivings about me, and what had occurred.

Mr. Kelly said he would talk to the sheriff about allowing me to have clean clothes and shower privileges so I could wash my hair and clean up occasionally. I begged him to bring me some books to read because I was losing my mind sitting in this small cage every day with no radio, no TV, and nothing to do but stare at the steel bars and concrete floors.

Since my cell was located in the center of the second-floor jail, I could not see out any window or get any sunshine. I felt like I was in a dark steel hole with no human contact or hope for the future.

I asked Mr. Kelly who prepared the food for the prisoners, since it was so lacking.

"The jailer and his wife live in the basement of the jail. She gets paid to prepare the daily meals for the prisoners," he replied.

Mr. Kelly had no idea what the future held for me, only that it appeared to be pretty grim.

He left, and I was alone with my thoughts. At least someone would feed and care for Butch; he certainly did not deserve to live like I was living. I was beginning to doubt my own sanity or ability to survive this ordeal.

My Church's preacher paid me a visit the next day. He was a young, pleasant man whom I had never met. He was uncomfortable with the surroundings, and after a few short pleasantries, he took his leave.

Mr. Kelly was able to talk the jailer into bringing me several old issues of *Reader's Digest*, which I read from cover to cover over the next few days.

The days began to drag by slowly and without any changes. The rats learned how lethal a hard thrown edition of *Reader's Digest* could be and started keeping a safe distance.

After several days with no contact from my court appointed lawyer, I began to realize that the local justice system had given me up for dead.

Mr. Kelly also began to notice and became alarmed by the lack of interest in my welfare by my lawyer and the local authorities.

"Bobby, I am going to find you a more concerned lawyer to look into your case; is that okay with you?" I gave him my whole-hearted support and thanks.

He also gave me the bad news about Butch, my pet.

"Butch has disappeared; even your neighbors have not seen him for several days."

The full impact of the deaths of my mother and sister now started hitting me like a blanket of doom. I went into a deep period of grieving that would last for months. Part of me died.

What little family I had was now gone, forever.

———

CHAPTER 22
A Little Hope

· · ·

SEVERAL DAYS LATER, THE JAILER came for me and said I had a room full of visitors downstairs. I followed him down the narrow staircase to the visitation room on the first floor of the jailhouse.

Mr. Kelly had evidently talked to another local attorney about my case and situation, and he had agreed to meet with me.

Hal Welch was a man about fifty or so. He had an air of confidence and no-nonsense about him. He introduced himself to me and said he and my court appointed lawyer wanted to talk to me in depth about what had happened on that fateful night. Vester Songer, my other attorney, was also there and seemed to show renewed interest in my case all of a sudden.

I knew Hal Welch by reputation. He was one of those lawyers who was a loner and did not care whose feelings he hurt or whose toes he stepped on in order to represent a client. I told the two lawyers what I knew about the night and about the recorded statement I gave to the agents. I told them that I really did not know or fully understand what had occurred that night, but I assured them I never had any intentions of harming my mother and sister and only wanted to have a career in the military.

Hal listened to my long and labored story without a word. When I finished, I had tears in my eyes. He looked at

Vester and said, "Looks like we need to get to work. This boy does not deserve this treatment. The first thing that needs to be done is to get him out of this jail and have some professional examine him."

"Keep your chin up, Bobby," Hal said. "Vester and I will not let you down."

I was also made aware for the first time that Agent Carmichael was actually not a law enforcement officer or an FBI agent; he was simply a paid investigator for the fire insurance industry. Of course, if I had burned down our house intentionally, no fire insurance claim would be paid.

They shook hands with me and left. The wheels of justice took another turn the next day. Motions were filed on my behalf and a different tone of legal proceedings occurred.

I was brought a change of clothes, soap, a razor, a mirror, and a comb, and was allowed to take a shower.

Two days later, I was taken before the same old county judge and adjudicated an adult since I was legally not an adult being under the age of twenty-one.

The judge also ordered I be transported to the Eastern State Hospital in Vinita, Oklahoma, for a full psychological and psychiatric evaluation. There were issues concerning my mental status.

It was common knowledge in our area of the state that all madmen and crazies were sent to Vinita, to the state asylum, so a chill went down my back when I heard where I was going. I guess everyone thought I was a crazy man.

"At least I won't have to fight rats off every night," I remarked to my lawyers, "And, hopefully the food improves."

The next day, one of the sheriff's deputies came for me, and we loaded into his squad car for the very long drive to Vinita, Oklahoma, at the northeast corner of the state. This was the same deputy I talked to at the hospital that Thursday morning, and he had been the one to drive me back home after the fire. I could tell he did not share the official line on this matter, and he allowed me to sit in the front seat with him, with no handcuffs. We talked about sports and the weather but avoided the circumstances of my case.

We stopped once at a truck stop for lunch, and he allowed me to stuff myself with food at the county's expense.

I could tell by the stares of the other customers in the restaurant that many recognized me from the photo that had appeared in almost every statewide newspaper. The onlookers kept whispering, "That's him. Where are his handcuffs?"

I really attracted attention when I excused myself to go to the restroom, leaving the deputy finishing his meal. I quickly returned and could see the relief on the deputy's face when he saw me coming. He and I both were quite aware I could have just gone out the back door and disappeared onto a passing eighteen-wheeler.

My freedom was quickly ended upon entry into the grounds of the state hospital. It was a scary looking place. I saw the large, ominous rows of brick buildings long before we arrived there. They looked like a backdrop for an Alfred Hitchcock movie: cold and forbidding. There was a high-security fence with guards around the perimeter. It really could have passed for a state prison; it basically was.

The guards at my building quickly took custody of me and sent the deputy on his way. They immediately put my arms and legs in shackles. I could barely walk. They took me up long stairs and down long hallways that were lined with hundreds of doors, each door having a face pressed against it to see who the new madman was. Evidently, news traveled fast in this institution, because all the staff and patients seemed to be expecting me.

I estimated I was on the fifth floor when the attendant opened one of the many doors and walked me into my new quarters, which consisted of a small foam mattress on the floor and a large light bulb in the center of the ceiling. There was a plastic bucket sitting in the corner. There was nothing else in the room: no furniture, no appliances, no bathroom, just a single mattress on the floor and the single strong light in the ceiling.

I was unshackled, and the door was locked as the attendant departed. I began to wonder if this was an improvement or not. At least there were no rats. I lay down on the mattress and really slept for the first night since my arrest.

A loud bang came from my door at exactly seven in the morning. I was handed a bowl of some type of tasteless cereal mush and a plastic spoon and told, "You have thirty minutes to eat and do your business in that bucket." Thankfully, the bucket had a lid on it.

They took my clothes and issued me a pair of pants and shirt clearly marked "State Hospital Inmate." At eight o'clock, the attendant opened the door and said to come with him. He took me to the end of the hallway to a large shower room and told me to strip naked and take a shower while he watched.

There were several older men already showering, and they showed great interest in my naked body while I washed my hair and showered. One of the younger men, about thirty years old, smiled at me and asked, "Bobby, what they got you for?"

"Suspicion of murder," I replied. I could tell he already knew who I was and why I was there.

"And you?" I asked, just to make conversation.

"Car theft." He grinned and under his breath said, "This place beats the hell out of the county jail, anytime."

"How long have you been here?" I asked.

"Two weeks, but I am trying to convince them I am crazy because I just got sentenced to ten years in the pen."

"Is everyone in this building a criminal suspect?" I asked.

"Yes, this is the criminally insane building. Lots of security and lots of head cases in here, so watch your back. Many of these crazies have nothing to lose, so they will hit or knife you without warning. My name is Jack; my half-brother is here with me, too—same charges as me. We are trying to buy time before that prison door slams in our face."

"Time's up!" the attendant yelled and took me back to my white walled cell. There was nothing to read or listen to, except a few screams occasionally.

That light bulb in my ceiling never turned off at night. It burned bright day or night. There was a small glass wire window about six inches by six inches in the entry room door so that the attendant could look into my room every thirty minutes or so to see what I was doing, which was not much. I would wave at him just to break the monotony.

The morning showers became my only social contact with the other patients. Since I was on the criminal floor, all these patients were either criminally insane or being evaluated to determine if they were criminally insane. Security was very strict, and no patient-to-patient contact was allowed.

Each day started with a shower and constant attendant supervision. Some days there might be ten or twelve grown men taking showers and shaving at the same time, and the noise could be considerable. Each man had been locked up for twenty-four hours with no one to talk to, so everyone talked at once. Some just sang songs; some were crazy out of their heads and just screamed and hollered. And some, like Jack, used the time to gather allies and pass information.

I had wondered why he immediately became friendly with me when most of the other men avoided me since I was branded a killer.

One large, wild-eyed character, who looked to be about thirty years old, immediately took a special interest in me, staring constantly. He supposedly had killed someone several years ago and was either insane or a good faker, because his eyes were wild and he often spit at the other patients and the attendants. He was built like a bulldog and was obviously strong and dangerous. He was usually content to talk to himself, but I noticed that he consistently stared at me while I showered. It was a little unnerving.

Jack always had news for me from the outside world and all the local hospital news and rumors. Somehow he managed to get himself connected to the hospital grapevine, and he was always full of new information.

He would inquire of me how long I had been in the county jail and if I really wanted to return. I shrugged and told him I was just doing what I was told.

"You know you are looking at many years in prison, don't you?" he would ask and closely watch my reaction. I avoided any direct responses and talked in general terms that I did not know what my future was.

He asked me what I could see out the back window of my room, and I saw no harm in describing that in detail. "Rooftops of the lower buildings," I would reply.

He seemed to have a clear view of certain parts of the hospital premises but not the parts that really interested him. He would often question other men in the shower about what they could see out of their room windows. I began to suspect he had a definite reason for trying to know exactly what could be seen from the windows on our floor.

After a couple of days, the attendant took me each day to a specialized room that was full of booths and various types of equipment. This was the room where the various types of psychological testing took place. For hours each day, doctors administered every type of test known to man, measuring every aspect of my being, conscious and unconscious. My eyes began to blur after a day of looking at inkblots and answering hundreds and hundreds of questions, both in writing and orally before technicians and psychologists.

Then came a week of staff meetings, whereby a team of psychologists and psychiatrists would drill me verbally for hours and hours, without a break, about the particulars of the crimes I was accused of committing. Their questions zeroed in on my relationship with my mother, my relationship with my sister, and my relationship with everybody involved in the episode.

After two weeks, I began to notice the doctors were asking the same questions they had asked a week earlier, seeing if they got the same answers again from me. They were very thorough.

The original court order sending me to the state hospital had stated the period of commitment could not exceed so many days.

I began to wonder if anyone who was left in this hospital for an extended period of time was in the same state of mind when they left. Many patients would scream all night, keeping the other patients awake. After eight hours of daily interrogations, I began to doubt my own sanity.

The third week began the physical tests; every kind of brain scan or test known to modern science was administered to me. Several of the technicians there should have worked in the Nazi death camps, because they certainly had that type of personality when handling the patients. A patient whose hands are chained to his side and whose feet are shackled is pretty helpless; a shove or shoulder bump could send that patient face first into the hard floor. It happened occasionally.

One day, I did not sit up fast enough to satisfy a female technician, who had me hooked up to a brain wave machine; she reached down and grabbed my privates with her hand and squeezed, hard, all the while with a big smile on her face. She was attractive, so I did not know if she was flirting with me or just a sadist—probably a little of both.

My stay in that hospital showed me first hand the mental illness treatments in common use, such as shock treatments. I would hear a male or female patient screaming non-stop for an hour or so, followed by a team of attendants pushing that patient down on his or her bed and restraining him or her and then bringing in the shock treatment equipment and sending electricity through the patient's brain. It certainly stopped the screaming.

Jack finally spilled the beans to me while we were talking one day in the shower. He was blunt. "Bobby, we are escaping tonight. Do you want to join?"

I had the shower water hitting me full in the face, and I almost drowned when he spoke so bluntly.

"What?" I managed to say. "You are going to escape? Why, you haven't a chance!"

He made sure no one could hear him, and he leaned closer. "I found a way out of this place, and we are going tonight. This place is like a sieve; a fool could escape. They are all fools."

I thought a minute and decided Jack was either playing me or he was a fool himself, because no one was going to escape this place, at least in my opinion.

"No, Jack, I can't, and I think you should reconsider. They will add five years to your sentence if you try to escape, and it is automatic."

Jack's reply was immediate. "I know, but it is the only chance we have before going to the big house."

That night, Jack and two others managed to escape; the hospital staff never mentioned a word about how they did it. I never saw him again.

Two days later, while taking my shower, the crazy guy made a lunge at me when the attendants were distracted. I was watching him and saw him coming and locked myself in one of the toilet stalls until five attendants could subdue him. He was locked away with no more shower privileges after that.

After a couple more days, the attendant brought me my old clothes and told me to get dressed. They were sending me back to the county jail. The doctors were finished with me and had prepared their final report.

It was a report the county attorney would not be happy with and which would surprise many of the people following my story.

———

CHAPTER 23
Home Again

• • •

WHEN I ARRIVED BACK AT the county jail from the state hospital, they put me into the bullpen with the other prisoners. I guess the report from Vinita assured the sheriff I was not a danger to others. In fact, the report took much wind out of the county attorney's case.

The report clearly stated that I had no evidence of an overt psychosis, and in their professional opinions, I had been truthful in all respects and had no memory of what caused the deaths of my mother and sister.

Since the report had been prepared by the state's own personnel, the state would now be reluctant to impeach it.

The local newspaper reported my return to the county jail to await trial and mentioned that I was found mentally competent. The newspaper did not give the *other* details of the report to the public.

The state was no longer in a hurry to bring the two murder cases to trial and seemed content to let me rot in the jail in the hope that time might solve the dilemma in which they found themselves.

The townspeople started to question the entire affair and wondered how a person who was now proven completely sane could suddenly one night decide to wipe out his entire family.

The bullpen had advantages and disadvantages. It was a fairly large area, probably the size of a two-bedroom home. It was one-half open area and one-half bunk beds with upper and lower single bed mattresses. It had one toilet to be shared by all and one water faucet and washbasin. The only shower was in the shower stall room, which was kept locked. The bullpen entrance connected with the room of the solitary confinement cells, where they had previously held me. The steel door entrance was so old a padlock and an old steel chain held it shut. Because the entrance door did not completely close and was only secured by a chain, there was about a three-inch open gap between the door and door frame. This allowed the jailer to hand small items to prisoners without having to unlock the door. This gap in the door, while certainly not wide enough for a prisoner to squeeze through, served as a never ending source of entertainment to the prisoners in the bullpen.

Any female prisoners were kept in the *open* solitary confinement cell area or cells in the adjoining room, where I had previously been confined. That door gap also provided just enough space to allow prisoners to pass contraband items back and forth to the jail *trustees*, who might be feeding prisoners or working in the adjoining room.

The bullpen had about twelve steel bunk beds along one side of the room and one toilet located exactly in front of the twelfth cell. Needless to say, no one wanted to be in that cell when someone was using that toilet. I soon learned that only the weak inherited that particular bunk bed next to the open toilet.

When I was first introduced to confinement in the bullpen, it was mostly empty. There were days when I was the only person there, but as time went by, the population slowly grew. On Friday and Saturday nights, the drunks and bar-fighters showed up all night. They were some of the worst. Some would be so drunk that as soon as the deputies shoved them into the bullpen, they collapsed on the floor, only waking up occasionally to vomit or pee or shit all over the place. They could never seem to find that one toilet at night, even with the occasional forceful persuasion of myself and other prisoners. The bar-fighters were the most dangerous. They had gotten drunk in a local bar and then decided to *kick some ass* and ended up in the county jail. The problem was, they were still drunk and wanting to kick ass—anyone's ass would do. If one of those fools stumbled into your bunk bed, you had to defend yourself as best you could or be beaten by a drunk who wouldn't remember a thing when he eventually sobered up. Usually a well placed fist to the chin or a cowboy boot kick in the face was enough to settle the character down for the night. In the morning, he would want to know who broke his nose or gave him a black eye. No one ever seemed to recall who that person was.

The drunks and fighters were usually bailed out or otherwise released on Monday morning, and things would quiet down until the following Friday night, and history would repeat itself. That routine never changed for me.

No one wanted to sleep on the top bunks for several reasons. If the person below was a drunk or mean and wanted to, they could kick the bottom of the bunk above them and send the person flying through the air and into a five foot drop onto a hard steel floor. Furthermore, the person with the bottom bunk could use the area under his bunk as his personal storage area to keep personal papers, snacks, and reading material. That was the only place for a prisoner to safely store his property. A long-term prisoner, such as me, soon learned to claim a bottom bunk and guard his personal items and area and advise others that the area was off limits to anyone else.

I had always been an easygoing, non-violent individual before I was jailed. I now had to learn how to defend myself, because the alternatives were not pleasant by any means.

Men who were locked up together, many of who were already bad elements, would quickly size up their fellow inmates and, within a short time, know who was weak and vulnerable and who not to mess with because he would not hesitate to kick in your face.

The prisoners were allowed to wear the clothes they were arrested in and keep a change of clothes in their bunks. The same applied to their footwear. Most men in this area wore boots, either work boots or cowboy boots. I soon learned that the preferred weapons of choice in the jail were boots, especially cowboy boots. A kick to the head or face can quickly take an opponent out of a fight. A kick in the stomach or kidney with a pointed cowboy boot can be life threatening and quickly end a fight.

The great advantage to kicking over fist fighting is that there is no evidence of busted hands or split knuckles afterward if the jailer tries to determine who hit whom.

I had to be very careful not to be named as an assault and battery defendant due to the likelihood the matter would become front page news in the local newspaper as further proof of my supposed criminal nature.

Most of the other jailed inmates knew who I was and with what I was charged and stayed away from me. That was fine with me because they were usually the dregs of society: burglary, robbery, and wife-beating suspects.

The bullpen had several standard size windows, which gave the prisoners views of the next door courthouse and views in two other directions, of neighborhood homes and streets. Of course, the windows had steel bars.

At least now I could perch in one of those windows and watch the people coming and going to the courthouse daily and watch the normal citizens going about their daily lives. Every now and then, I would even see some of my high school buddies drive by in their Chevys and Fords. Occasionally, one would honk his horn as a signal I was not completely forgotten.

One day, I was startled and excited when I saw a dog I was sure was Butch standing in the front yard of a house across the street from the jail. He just stood there, seemingly unsure where he was. He stared at the jail as if he knew I was there. He looked ragged and poorly fed. He suddenly ran away behind the houses when a woman hollered at him from the front porch.

My heart was pounding. I remembered that Butch disappeared from my burned home a week or so after I was arrested, and I assumed someone had taken him to care for. I watched the area for the remainder of the day, but he never reappeared. Over the next several weeks, I would catch glimpses of him across the street from the jail, and then he would disappear again.

Mr. Kelly did his best to stay in contact with me and brought me books to read and tried to keep my sagging spirits up.

One day, I noticed great activity at the courthouse as the employees and others ran to their vehicles. I heard someone shout, "The president has been shot."

The courthouse was soon empty and locked down for the day as everyone left to watch their televisions. The jailer told us when he served supper that night that President Kennedy was dead, shot by an assassin, and Lyndon Johnson was our new president. The event saddened everyone in jail, and we wished for more details of what was happening in the outside world. We had no TV, but several prisoners had transistor radios, which played until everyone's batteries were dead.

It became even more depressing in the jail as the holiday season arrived. With it came a noticeable increase in the jailing of drunks and bar-fighters. Soon the jail bullpen was full, and each bunk bed was claimed at night.

A teenage Negro youth was arrested on suspicion of a minor theft charge. This was the first black male who had been placed in the bullpen up to that time. He was about my age and scared to death when he realized he was the only black person in a jail full of about twenty white guys. A few drunken Indians got thrown in from time to time, but they were usually released as soon as they sobered up.

The other white prisoners made it clear to the black kid that he was not welcome to sleep in their bunk beds.

It finally became apparent that my top bunk bed was his last resort, and I told him he could sleep there as long as he stayed away from my personal property under my bunk. That seemed to defuse the situation, and after a few days, the jailer made the kid his trustee to peel potatoes and help his wife with the cooking. The prisoners passed the hat and collected a few dollars and begged the kid to buy some seasonings for the pinto beans and boiled potatoes, which he did. The food improved in the sense it had some seasonings in it now.

I was quite surprised to see the jailer's wife was very attractive, a well built blonde woman in her late twenties. There were two clotheslines outside one side of the jail, and once a week she washed her clothes and hung them out to dry on those two clotheslines. It became quite an event to us prisoners. The wife would put on skintight short-shorts and a skimpy halter-top and parade up and down those clotheslines much of the day. She obviously enjoyed driving all of us crazy.

She would slowly bend over with her butt in our direction as she picked up clothes to hang. Even catcalls from some of the more slow-witted prisoners did not deter her. She always wore the same clothes, even in the cold weather. I am sure the jailer had his hands full having her for a wife. The prisoners often remarked the jailer must have something special to attract such a striking blonde as her. The jailer's salary was very modest, and they lived in the basement of the jail, so it was always a source of wonderment to us what she saw in the brute she had married.

With the approaching Christmas came more parties, and the deputies even started bringing in drunken women occasionally. One such cowgirl proved to be quite a character. It was a Saturday night at about midnight when we heard a woman screaming so loud that I am sure it woke up everyone within a block of the jail. The two deputies that brought her to the jail had handcuffed and shackled her in order to control her. We saw them unload her from the squad car and hand her over to the jailer. The deputies drove away quickly.

The jailer brought her up the stairs to the second floor cells, which were next to the bullpen, and took her shackles off. She promptly kicked him and cursed him and all his relatives. He told her he was going to leave her in handcuffs if she did not settle down. She got very quiet. As soon as the cuffs were off, she screamed, "He is trying to rape me! Get your hands off my tits." The jailer was well aware his wife could hear this exchange downstairs and tried to back out the door and get away from her. She kept screaming and started taking off her clothes and was soon completely naked. She was very well built.

"Come fuck me, you worthless pig!" she hollered.

By now all the prisoners in the bullpen were stacked up at the bullpen cell door, watching this melodrama unfold through the three-inch gap that separated the chained door from the wall.

The totally naked girl, very proud of herself, tried to grab the jailer, but he ducked and slammed and locked the cell door and fled down the stairs.

She could see all the men's faces looking through the gap at her, and she walked over so everyone could get a closer look at her assets, which were considerable. She turned her butt to the door and bent over and said, "It's Christmas and here is your present, so come get it."

She backed her butt up to the crack in the door. Several men immediately dropped their pants and brought out their equipment, but no one had a long enough tool to make contact with her vital area. After much moaning and groaning and cussing, it became apparent that such a connection was not going to work. Suddenly, the black kid announced he had the necessary equipment to handle the project and showed everyone what he had to offer. Two of the white men threatened to kill him on the spot for messing with a white woman. The kid backed away and pulled up his pants.

The wild girl was getting pretty frustrated by now with the inadequateness of the men and turned around to the door and put her face to the crack and announced she would give each and every man—except, of course, the black guy—a good blowjob.

The line formed quickly, and she went to work with a flourish. She was quite skilled with her mouth and soon had men screaming and thanking Jesus for their Christmas present.

When it came my time, I declined, to everyone's amazement.

"What's the problem, Bobby? Don't you like girls?"

"Yes, I do, but has anyone noticed that if she suddenly decided to slam that cell door closed, they would lose their dick!" I exclaimed.

Several of the prisoners said a little prayer of thanks, and that was the end of the lovemaking for the night. But it would not be the last time that a drunken woman, or sometimes a sober woman, gave pleasure to the men in the bullpen through that small gap.

Some of the prisoners, especially the ones who had done prison time, knew all the tricks of making life a little more comfortable while imprisoned

Each prisoner was allowed to keep a small amount of cash at the sheriff's office. This was money deposited by friends and family of the prisoner. Mr. Kelly had made a deposit with the sheriff so I could buy toiletries and snacks.

The prisoners would give the black trustee a list of what they wanted him to buy for them, and he would purchase it with the prisoners' funds and deliver the items to the prisoners, who would usually share some of it with the trustee as a reward for his efforts.

Coffee, candies, and other foodstuffs, mostly canned, would be purchased and eaten by the prisoners to supplement their meager jail meals. Prisoners built a crude cook stove; they put a roll of toilet paper inside and lit it. A roll of toilet paper burns very slowly with no smell or smoke, and the prisoners could boil coffee and other foodstuffs without the jailer having a clue.

While looking through my meager personal belongings one day I noticed the old envelope with my father's last known address in Eureka, California. I spent hours composing a handwritten letter to him asking him to come to my rescue. I described in detail what had happened, placed the letter in an envelope, gave it to the trustee, and paid him to take it to the post office a block away and buy a stamp and mail it for me. I put a return address on the envelope to me at the county jail. The next day he swore he mailed it for me. I never received any response from my father. That letter would become very important later when it was returned, unopened, to the sheriff, and he opened and read it.

So, here I lay, on my old, smelly, cotton mattress, and I still had no clear memory of those last moments before I was found in the wet field next to my burning home.

I could only remember going to bed as usual and being startled from a deep sleep in the early morning hours by my screaming mother standing over me and holding one of my loaded rifles pointed directly at my face. I knew I had to get that rifle barrel out of my face quickly or I would die. That was my last conscious thought before I was shaken in the wet field by a neighbor shouting, "Bobby, what happened?"

I could not recall any other memory lapses in my lifetime, except not remembering anything before my father walked out on us many years before.

Everything that had happened to my family that morning was just one giant puzzle to me.

———

CHAPTER 24

Daylight Hope

• • •

I AWOKE ONE MORNING AND was shocked to see the jail door standing open and everyone gone. I walked down that one flight of stairs to the outside of the jail, and there was my dog, Butch, and my old pickup truck waiting for me with the keys in the ignition. I got in, and Butch hopped in beside me, and off we drove. In a few blocks, I noticed my old friend, George, hitchhiking, and picked him up. He was wearing an army uniform, and I was immediately jealous.

"Where have you been, and when did you join the army?" I asked and looked at his pale face and blank eyes.

"Away, far away. Why are you in jail, Bobby? You have done no harm to anyone," was his faraway reply.

"I know that, but others doubt me. I am in serious trouble," I said.

"You are going to be fine. Everything will be resolved. You just have to be strong." His voice started to fade.

And then I awoke with a start, sweating and quite shaken. I looked around and soon realized it had all been a dream, a very strange dream, more than a normal dream—some kind of supernatural message to me from an unknown source. The vividness of the dream remained with me forever. There was a message being sent to me, either from my subconscious mind or some outside force. I have never known for sure what it was all about and probably never will, but it became a source of inner strength and peace to me. Maybe there was an end to my nightmares in sight.

The Christmas and New Year's holiday came and went. My routine menu stayed the same. Mr. Kelly brought me some Christmas cookies and encouragement that things could only get better. I had my doubts.

One day in January 1964, the jailer brought two new prisoners to the bullpen. They looked and acted different than the usual crowd of riff-raff that came through that revolving door.

The two men were in their late twenties, well dressed and clean-cut. They wore expensive loafers and custom haircuts. They stayed together and had nothing to say to the other prisoners. The rumor was they were professional safecrackers from up North who had the misfortune of being stopped for speeding in our city. The deputies noticed their out-of-state plates and asked them to open their car trunk, and they had refused. The deputies opened it anyway and found what appeared to be stolen items. They refused to answer the deputies' questions and were promptly jailed.

Over the next few days, the bullpen emptied out until there was only the two of them, James, the trustee, and me.

The most popular method of passing the time in jail was playing dominos, especially the game Moon. It took four players to play the game properly. Therefore, the two strangers teamed against James and me in some serious dominos duels. James mentioned to them I had formally worked in the town's grocery store. The two strangers suddenly began asking me questions about the location of the store's burglar alarms and where the safe was located. I instantly knew why they were passing through our town. They had been casing that grocery store and were planning to break in and crack the store safe. My immediate reaction to their questions was, "You do not want to touch that store; it has a hidden burglar alarm system wired directly to the local police station, which is only a block away. You guys would not stand a chance of getting away."

They exchanged looks of concern, and the subject did not come up again. They thereafter became quite friendly with me and shared their snacks, coffee, and other extras that they obtained through James' efforts.

In truth, I knew the grocery store where I had worked was a burglar's delight. No security, no alarm systems, and an old cracker-barrel safe, probably stuffed full of cash. I just felt a loyalty to my old manager and the store's owner. They both had always been fair to me and provided me a place to work. I would have never done anything to betray their trust in me.

A day later, another stranger was introduced into the jail. He was a big man, with a big mouth to match. He supposedly had been arrested for not paying his child support obligations. That struck me as a little suspicious, because he was the only man I knew of who was ever jailed for not paying child support. He was about forty years old.

He immediately tried to befriend me for some unknown reason, but I rebuffed his advances. He came into my cell bunk late one night and whispered that we needed to talk. His face got closer and closer to my face. When I had no more room to lean back, he tried to kiss me on the lips. I had a hardback novel in my right hand and hit him in the face as hard as possible. The blood poured from his nose and mouth, and he cussed and ran out of my cell, holding his face.

The next day, things were very tense in the bullpen. He sat on his bunk bed and called me every name in the book but a white man. He cursed me to the point I could not ignore it anymore, and I finally lost my patience and slapped him across the face. He then lunged for me, and suddenly the two safecrackers jumped between us, and the smaller one, who was only five feet four and only weighed about one-hundred and forty pounds, hit the man very hard between the eyes with his right fist. The attacker stood there stunned for a moment and looked at the shorter man like he was going to get the beating of his life. In the meantime, the other safecracker, a larger man about six foot and weighing probably one hundred and eighty pounds, spun the attacker around and pinned both his arms behind his back. He then spun the guy back around to face the shorter man, who proceeded to pound the attacker's face with both fists until his face was a bloody mess. Then they released him, and the attacker collapsed on the floor, unconscious and badly beaten. Obviously, the two safecrackers had done this before and performed like a two-man wrecking ball, without even breathing hard.

They turned to me and said, "Bobby, this guy was *planted* here to get information from you or get you in trouble for fighting. We knew it when he walked in the door. You need to watch for those scumbags. You did us a favor, so we did you a favor. Don't get in any trouble while you are in this jail or the state will use it against you when you go to trial."

I shook their hands and thanked them for their advice. The two safecrackers were released the next day for lack of evidence, and they quickly departed the area, never to be heard from again.

A week later, I mentioned to RD, my old manager, that I had discouraged some potential burglars from breaking into the grocery store safe and suggested they upgrade their security, since the next safecrackers to happen into town might take advantage of the easy pickings.

A few weeks later, my lawyers advised me that the owner of that grocery store and another man had offered to post a bail bond for me if one could be arranged. That was the first time the possibility of a bail bond for me had been discussed seriously.

Several other unrelated events in the county had also raised questions as to why no bail bond had been ever set for me.

One event was when a local rancher caught his wife and his best friend making love at a local motel. The rancher pulled his .38 pistol and shot them both to death in their motel bed. He calmly waited for the sheriff, who knew the shooter. The sheriff released the man on a personal recognizance bond. He was never even jailed.

Another double shooting took place in town a few weeks later, with similar facts and circumstances. Again, the local sheriff released the accused local businessman on a personal recognizance bond. He was never jailed.

People in town started talking and wondering if maybe there were two standards of justice in town, one for the people of means and another for a local teenage boy who had no money and no relatives.

The county attorney was opposed to bail but was obviously in no hurry to bring the two murder cases to trial, so my lawyers requested my release on bail. The judge ordered a fifty thousand dollar bail. The grocery store owner and a local deacon from my church immediately arranged the required bail-bond.

I was now a free man for the first time in eight months. I had a few changes of clothes, but no home, no relatives, no car, and no job, and about forty-three dollars to my name. But I was *free* at last—thank God almighty, free at last.

Losing one's freedom and being locked up and treated like some kind of animal is a shock to a person in and of itself, but to a country boy like myself, who was used to being free to roam the woods, fields, and streams at will, my confinement was especially difficult. I would never again enjoy going to a zoo and watching confined animals, because I knew how imprisonment really felt and why they constantly paced their cells, like caged men do. I spent eight months in jail and had never been convicted of anything.

CHAPTER 25

Freedom

• • •

I WAS UTTERLY LOST WHEN I was released from jail: nowhere to go, no job, no more routine, and no direction. I spent the first day wandering around town, just looking at everything like a wide-eyed kid.

Mr. Kelly checked me into a cheap hotel so I would have a place to sleep that first night and invited me to eat supper with his family. The local Christian church deacon who co-signed my bail bond offered me lunch the next day at his house, which I accepted with gratitude.

My first mission as a free man was to try to locate Butch. I walked the neighborhood where I had last seen him, but I had no luck. I then started to knock on doors. Several people said they had seen Butch in the neighborhood, and he seemed confused, hungry, and lost. Some had even fed and watered him. Finally, I located someone who was willing to tell me the truth. The old gentleman said, "Son, your poor dog is dead. I buried him. One of my damn neighbors poisoned him because he would not stay out of her yard. I am sorry. I knew he was someone's pet, and he just could not find his home."

A very large lump rose in my throat. I thanked him for his efforts. It all made sense now as to why Butch had suddenly disappeared from view a few weeks ago. Butch was the last piece remaining of my previous life, and he would be irreplaceable in my heart and mind. Another part of me was now dead.

Mr. Kelly announced that night that he would help me find a job. There was no use looking locally due to my notoriety. He thought my best hope was to relocate to Paris, Texas, about thirty miles away, where people would not know or recognize me. He had a connection at a large lumber company in Paris, and the next afternoon, he loaded my stuff and me in his vehicle, and we drove to Paris. He talked the general manager into hiring me as a yard worker, loading and unloading lumber trucks and making deliveries.

The manager cautioned me that it was hard physical labor and most white guys did not stay long. His current yard crew of four black men had been with him for years and might feel threatened by him hiring a new white guy.

I told him I was just excited to get to work outside in the fresh air and would make him a good hand. He handed me a pair of leather gloves and introduced me to the store personnel, and I went to work for one dollar per hour for a forty-five hour workweek. Mr. Kelly found me a nearby small, furnished apartment to rent for twenty dollars a week. I had no vehicle, so I could either ride the city bus or walk to work. I was ready to start my new life.

I had done no physical work for eight months, and the work of a yardman in a busy lumberyard was hard and backbreaking. But I loved it, and as it turned out, I loved it too much. The four black workers grew hostile because I was too eager to quickly load and unload truckloads of lumber, cement, and concrete blocks. They constantly told me to slow down; I was making them look bad. The oldest and friendlier Negro, Leroy, who was the outside yard manager, told me that the other three workers were afraid I was trying to replace one of them, and each of them had families to support. I assured Leroy I only wanted to be a good worker and had no interest in taking anyone's job. But I also saw trouble coming, and that I certainly did not need.

I started to use Saturday afternoons to try to locate another, hopefully better paying job. I applied at a locally owned grocery store for a meat-cutting job. The store manager said he really needed a meat department manager who was also a skilled meat cutter. I told him I could manage his meat department and do all the meat cutting myself. He was unsure a nineteen-year old had enough experience for such a job. But he was desperate and offered me the job. He told me to be at work Monday morning at seven o'clock. The pay was two dollars per hour. I called the general manager at the lumber company, and he was glad to hear the news, because he said he was under pressure from the other yard workers to "do something with me."

I was excited to return to work at which I was skilled. I soon had the store's meat market in excellent shape, and the customers started to compliment the store manager on the improvement in the meat market and the nice young man working there.

The store manager was almost seventy years old but had been a meat cutter earlier in his work life, and he knew I was very skilled and ran a clean, smooth operation. He contacted the owner of the store, who owned and managed another grocery store in Farmersville, Texas, about fifty miles away. He told the storeowner about the quality of my work, and the owner drove down to meet and talk with me.

The owner said he needed a meat department manager at his Farmersville store also and asked me to spend the coming weekend with him and his family and try to shape up his grocery store's meat market, which supposedly was a mess.

I told him I had no vehicle, and he said he would drive me to Farmersville and bring me back to Paris. I would be working all weekend at his meat market, trying to bring it up to par with the one in Paris, Texas. The weekend went well.

So I started working seven days per week, five in Paris managing that meat department, and two days in Farmersville, managing that meat department. That was fine with me, and I was soon saving money to purchase a used vehicle so I could have some transportation.

The owner of the two stores welcomed me into his home and treated me like one of his sons. His very attractive seventeen-year old daughter and I made eyes at each other. I slept in one of his spare bedrooms while working at his store location and ate all my meals at the family table.

Life was great for a few weeks; I had both meat markets shaped up and profitable in a month and as clean as any hospital operating room. The owner was amazed and thrilled. And then reality reared its ugly head one afternoon while I was working in the Paris store. A local deputy sheriff was shopping with his wife in that store, and I was preparing a crown roast for a special occasion for her when her husband suddenly recognized me. In front of a store full of customers, he pointed at me and loudly proclaimed for all to hear, "You are Bobby Wilson, from Hugo, Oklahoma, aren't you?" I froze. "When did you get out of jail?"

I died inside. The old store manager was working with a customer at the front of the store, and I saw him promptly turn around and stare at me and reach for the phone. I knew who he was calling.

That night, the owner drove into town to meet with me and tell me it probably would be better if I moved on, but he thanked for my efforts on behalf of his two businesses.

The old store manager refused to even talk to me again. I gathered my property and final paycheck and retreated to my small apartment to feel sorry for myself.

The next day, I packed up my few items, purchased a used vehicle, settled up with my landlord, and drove to Dallas, Texas, to try to find another job.

I applied at the district office of Safeway Stores for a meat cutter position and was hired on the spot and told to appear for work at a certain store across town.

I was finally able to locate that particular store in this very large city. I had not been in a large city since moving to Oklahoma, and Dallas was very overwhelming to me—too many people, cars, and streets for this country boy.

I found the housing possibilities for a single fellow my age very limited. I learned that most single men lived in rooming homes where a bedroom was rented by the week or month and the owner furnished the tenant a full breakfast and supper each day. This type of set up seemed to be the most practical short-term solution, so I located one such three-story rooming house. The landlady, a self-assured divorcee of about fifty, showed me the third floor bedroom, explained the host of non-negotiable rules of her house, and demanded full rent in advance. One of her clear rules was no drinking or womanizing and a curfew of eleven o'clock each night.

"The front door is locked at eleven o'clock each night and unlocked at six o'clock in the morning. If you are not in that front door by eleven, you are not getting in until six in the morning," she explained forcefully.

I could tell that she did not stand for any violations of her rules.

All new hires in the Dallas Safeway Stores meat departments had a ninety day probation period for determination of whether you could satisfactorily perform their work assignments and a determination of your skill level. There was a big difference in pay between an apprentice meat cutter and a journeyman meat cutter. In thirty days, the manager of my assigned store certified me to the district manager that my skill level was that of a journeymen meat cutter, and my wages were raised to about three dollars an hour, plus full employment benefits.

I was also placed in their management training program for rapid advancement. My quick advancements on the jobsite were matched with my continuing problems of learning the streets and neighborhoods of Dallas. I often got lost, especially at night, trying to find my way around Dallas.

One night, I had worked at my store until ten o'clock and tried to take a short cut to my rooming house since I needed to be there no later than eleven. I became hopelessly lost on the dark and winding streets of Northeast Dallas. By the time I finally found my rooming house, it was almost midnight and all the lights were off and the front door locked. I did not dare knock on that door. I looked at the huge elm trees around the side of the house and noticed the low hanging limbs. If I could reach the second story roof, I could climb to my bedroom window on the third floor and gain entry through the unlocked window. That was a better idea.

I quietly climbed the elm tree and lowered myself nimbly onto the second story roof and made my way around toward the back part of the house where I could climb to the third floor roof. As I crawled past one of the second-story windows, I noticed a dim light shining within that bedroom and could not help seeing a fully naked man and woman engaged in passionate lovemaking. I froze as I recognized my landlady as the woman and another tenant about my age as the man.

My movement caught her eye, and I heard her yell. I ducked and rapidly climbed to the third floor, opened my bedroom window, dropped into my room, and quickly removed my clothes. I jumped in bed in the darkened room and covered my head with the covers.

"Mr. Wilson, you awake?" the landlady asked as she opened my bedroom door.

I mumbled, "What? Who is it?"

"Some peeping Tom is crawling around on our roof. Have you seen or heard anything?"

"No, ma'am!" was my quick reply. "Do you want me to get dressed and look for him?"

"No, I will let it go this time." She shut the door.

The next day, I bought a City of Dallas map and always kept it in my vehicle thereafter.

On my days off from work I would drive to nearby Love Field Airport and watch the big jet planes land and take off. I was still fascinated by airplanes.

During my high school days I had entirely focused my efforts on becoming a career army military officer. I never considered any alternative career choices. I had read every book on military people, places, and events that I could locate and was an expert on the military history of the United States.

Now, with felony cases pending against me, no military recruiter would be interested in me. I had to support myself the best way I could until this ordeal ended.

———

CHAPTER 26

Trial Preparation

• • •

WITH THE TRIAL DATE APPROACHING, my lawyer notified me they had obtained a well-known and respected doctor of psychiatry in Oklahoma City, who had agreed to see me for the purposes of evaluation. The lawyers were very concerned because I was still unable to advise them as to facts surrounding my family's deaths. The lawyers needed more proof than just my testimony as to why I could not recall those terrible events.

I made arrangements to leave my workplace for several days and drove to Oklahoma City to the good doctor's offices.

The doctor had an impressive office and testing facilities. I spent the first day undergoing all types of psychological written tests and the second day answering questions from him and his staff. It was a condensed version of the weeks of testing I went through at the state hospital in Vinita, Oklahoma.

On my drive back to Dallas, I stopped and met with my lawyers, and they drilled me for hours about the facts of the case and stated, "How are we going to defend you when you cannot tell us what happened and why it happened?"

I added to their frustration with my response: "I do not know what happened; the only thing I know for sure is that I would never have harmed my family."

The trial date finally arrived in March of 1965. I was told to be in the district court of the county courthouse in Hugo, Oklahoma, for jury selection on that date. It was a surreal drive from my new home in Dallas back to the town I now had mixed feelings about.

Hugo was a town of about six thousand residents, founded in 1902 and named after the French writer, Victor Hugo. It is the county seat of Choctaw County, Oklahoma. It is located in the southeastern part of the state, near the Red River, and only twenty-five miles from Paris, Texas.

The Frisco Railroad lines were built in 1902 and brought life to Hugo, along with plenty of newcomers, outlaws, and gunfighters. Choctaw County came into existence in 1907, when statehood came to Oklahoma. There was a heavy American Indian presence at the time, and the tribal name of Chahta was to become Choctaw. The county courthouse and county jail were built in 1913.

Potential jurors packed the courthouse, and from them the lawyers would select twelve to decide my fate.

The tension in the air in the courtroom was palpable, and everyone stared at me. There were other cases on the docket that day, but the judge quickly disposed of them, and the main event was clearly the two murder charges pending against me. The state loudly announced its intention to try both cases involving my mother and sister's deaths first.

The county attorney, Ralph Jenner, pranced around the front of the courtroom, holding his suspenders with both hands and exchanging greetings to the potential jurors who now completely packed the rows of bleacher seats behind the counsel tables. Jenner nodded to my two lawyers and made a big production of walking over to where I sat, wearing my one and only cheap suit. He asked in his loud, slow drawl, "Bobby, how are you doing?"

Hal Welch, my new lawyer, sprang to his feet and loudly shouted for all to hear, "Don't talk to that boy again! Not now or ever—understand?"

It was suddenly very quiet in the courtroom. Jenner took his seat like a scolded child and looked at the ceiling, his face very red.

It was now clear to all that the state's steamroller had hit a big bump in the road, and it was time for the prosecutor to prove his allegations against me without the help of the local press.

Two other unlikely events occurred when I returned home for this trial.

Judy, my old girlfriend, suddenly appeared. I had not heard anything from her or seen her since the night she had tearfully left the county attorney's interrogation room scared half to death that she was a criminal suspect in this matter. I had heard she had quickly moved away. I was startled to see her standing against the far back wall of the packed courtroom. She gestured for me to come to the back of the courtroom and speak to her.

I mentioned her presence to my lawyers, and they told me to take her into the empty jury room and see what she wanted, since it might be important. The court was not yet in official session, so I motioned to her to meet in the jury room. I held the door open for her, and before I could close it behind us, she threw her arms around me and kissed me passionately, and her tears started flowing.

"I still love you so much," she sobbed.

I held her and tried to console her while looking through the still partially open door. I was concerned about the potential jurors watching this display of emotions.

"What do you want?" I asked, trying to be as businesslike as possible.

"I want to see you, Bobby—soon!" her voice was starting to rise.

"Okay," I said, "But where do you live?"

She handed me a piece of paper that had her out-of-town address and her phone number.

"Call before you come, because my husband is home on the weekends. He is a long-haul truck driver and gone all week."

I remained calm and did not show my shock at her response. I asked her, "Is there anything else you need to tell me?"

There was not, so I told her she should not stay around the courthouse or someone might subpoena her. She agreed and left promptly. I never saw her or my class ring again.

Another woman from my past appeared. The cute brunette I had dated for a while who used to shop with her mother every Saturday at my place of employment now worked at the courthouse. I had seen and talked to her several times as I had come back and forth to the courthouse but had never asked her out. I did not want to embarrass her or her parents by having their daughter dating the most infamous man in town. But we did become friendly again, and she followed the events of my trial closely. I wanted her to, because she would soon learn that that most of the information printed in the newspapers about me had been false or misleading in nature and that this was a much more complicated story than had been portrayed in the press.

———

CHAPTER 27

Trial One

• • •

A CRIMINAL JURY TRIAL CONDUCTED under American law is quite similar to a professional hockey game in which two teams of professionals line up against each other before judges and fans and see which team can score the most points. In an American criminal trial, the accused defendant serves as the puck. If the so-called presumption of innocence rule of law was strictly followed in American courtrooms, the defendant would not even need to show up or put on a defense unless the prosecutor had already proven his case beyond a reasonable doubt to the judge.

A trial court judge is charged with the duty to dismiss a criminal case against a defendant when the state or prosecutor has failed to prove each element of the charge and has rested its case and before the defendant introduces any evidence. Most judges do not have the intestinal fortitude to carry out their sworn duty and will simply order the case be submitted to the jury for determination and let the jury take the public heat if the verdict is controversial. Submission of an iffy criminal case to a jury is a violation of the law, but it occurs every day in American courtrooms. There is great danger of a miscarriage of justice if a judge allows an unproven criminal case to be thrown into the lap of jurors who are more concerned about how their family and neighbors are going to react to their verdicts than they are concerned about the defendant's rights to justice and freedom.

The judge must act as the judicial gatekeeper and not allow a foggy or unproven criminal case to be submitted to a jury whose sworn duty is to only find a defendant guilty if the proof submitted proves those facts beyond a reasonable doubt. If a reasonable doubt exists in the judge's mind at the time he submits a criminal case to a jury, then he has failed to carry out his sworn duty, even if it may not have been a politically popular decision for the judge to make. That is his job, and he chooses to perform it. And while a defendant has no obligation to testify at his own criminal trial, the jury expects him to do so, and very few defendants win acquittals unless they do take the stand in their own defense.

In order to be convicted of murder in Oklahoma, the state prosecutor must prove that the defendant, with "malice aforethought," caused an unlawful death of a human—in other words, the defendant planned to kill someone in cold blood.

Second-degree murder has slightly less burden for the prosecutor; he must prove the defendant's murderous conduct was done intentionally and the defendant was of depraved mind and acting in extreme disregard of human life with the intent to kill.

If the prosecutor rests his case of murder against a defendant without offering sufficient proof of each of the elements required by state law to prove a murder took place, then the defendant's Motion for Directed Verdict should be granted as a matter of law and the defendant discharged—case over.

But most judges do not want the attention of siding with a defendant in a criminal trial, due to the political ramifications, so it is much easier for a judge just to overrule the defendant's Motion for Directed Verdict and move the trial forward to conclusion and submission to a jury of legally untrained minds.

Many potential jurors have been heard to say, "I will wait until I hear both sides before I make up my mind," or, "I heard the state's side; now I want to hear the defense side." Both these comments, and similar ones, mean the juror is not giving the defendant the presumption of innocence and is requiring proof of his innocence. While that is just human nature, it is a violation of a juror's oath. As one old hardheaded German farmer once said while being the lone juror to dissent in an eleven-to-one vote for acquittal on a murder case, "The defendant must be guilty, or he would not be on trial!"

How can you argue with logic like that?

My trial date in March 1965 would start with the selection of an *impartial jury*. That process was difficult and exhausting for all involved. The local newspaper coverage of the *two murders* had been widespread and very convincing as to my guilt in the matter. Most potential jurors were quite frustrated by the trial's interference with more important pursuits, such as their jobs, homes, families, and farms, especially when they believed the defendant had already given a full, signed confession that had been printed in the local newspaper. Why was such a waste of everyone's time and the county's money so necessary?

The presiding judge, Honorable Howard Phillips, instructed the courtroom full of jurors about their responsibilities as officers of the court and asked if any potential jurors had preconceived opinions as to the guilt or innocence of the defendant. Several hands were quickly raised.

Yes, they had opinions and they could not be fair.

They were excused. This encouraged others who just did not want to be there in the first place to suddenly announce their preconceived opinions of guilt or innocence. No one in the courtroom really believed that any of the excused jurors thought I was innocent, but everyone had to give that idea lip service at the very least.

It took two days to select twelve good people from the community to serve on that jury. The prosecutor made his opening statement describing in stark terms the brutal deaths of my mother and sister and how overwhelming the evidence was against "young Wilson, seated there."

The trial finally got underway with a sheriff's deputy, the three government agents (well, not quite, as it turned out— actually, two state investigators and an arson investigator paid by the fire insurance company), and various other witnesses who testified to their versions of the evidence.

It was never disputed that my mother died of a single bullet wound to the head, Sister died from a blow to her head, and the house burned, along with my nearby, parked Ford pickup truck, but then things got complicated.

Nobody disputed I had worked all week at the grocery store from open to close, driving there and back home in my Ford pickup each day without incident.

No one disputed my story that my mother woke me early in the morning and pointed a loaded rifle in my face. There was no testimony concerning my sister's involvement in any of these factors, or how she became involved, if she did.

No one disputed that the house burned.

No one could explain why I had taken the supposed murder weapon, a broken .22 caliber rifle, out of the house, the same rifle my mother had pointed at me with threats to kill.

No one could explain why, if I planned such a series of events or was acting with a guilty mind, I did not just leave the broken rifle in the house to be destroyed and why, the same day of the fire, I drove to my mother's rental house next door to where she worked and, in broad daylight, asked the renters if I could store my personal belongings in their storage building. Not exactly a clear pattern of criminal intent on my behalf.

One helpful witness for the state, a Deputy Sheriff Doyle, had even volunteered that I told him I didn't have enough gasoline stored in the house to do the job but had actually drained gasoline out of my pickup truck so I could really soak down the house interior with gasoline before standing inside and striking a match. Of course, it was all a lie.

Agents Carmichael and Stringer were arson experts by training and experience and knew full well that a closed house in which gasoline had been poured around would be so full of explosive gasoline fumes that *no one* standing within that house would have survived the blast and flaming explosion. It would have been certain death for me.

Neither of them bothered to testify to those facts, since it was more convincing for the state to stand on its theory that I just burned the house to cover a double homicide.

Another factor in the case that was like the elephant in the room that no one talked about was my relationship with my sister. The state's only theory was that she must have died after my mother's death, but they had no proof of that. The state's own evidence was that my mother's actions that night were the start of the confrontation leading to the deaths and fire.

So why would I kill my sister? No one had an answer for that question. There was no evidence that I had ever been anything but a loyal, loving, hardworking son and brother. I had no motive or reason to harm my sister; this was the weakest point in the state's case, and they knew it and avoided the issue as much as possible.

I never told anyone I had shot my mother or hit my sister, and I really did not have any memory of how the fire started. I only told the agents there were two gallons of gasoline in closed glass containers in the corner of my room and several closed glass containers of kerosene in the attic of the house. Everything else about the fire was conjecture and lies.

In answer to questions about what had occurred that night, I simply said, "I was the only one still alive, so I guess I did everything, but I really do not remember anything after Mother stuck the rifle in my face and threatened to shoot me."

One witness testified that my mother came by their house that very day before the deaths and loudly pronounced, "There will be hell at my house tonight; Bobby is hiding his pickup from me."

The significance of that statement is great. It meant that mother was planning a major confrontation with me that very night and that she was insane, because I had been driving that pickup truck back and forth all week to the grocery store where I was working, and she had always had a set of keys to the pickup. So how could *anyone* think I was hiding my truck from her?

This very crucial piece of evidence had been known from the date of the fire by the sheriff and investigation agents; but they had never shared this information with the news media or even my attorneys and me. Such information would have cast a completely different tone to the news coverage, since it showed conclusively that my mother was the attacker, not me.

Several other witnesses testified to confrontations with my mother in which she had threatened them physically or with death. The man who sold my mother our farm and his brother also took turns as witnesses. Another man was the man who sold her the '59 Ford a year earlier.

It was clear by the end of the trial that my mother was the irrational member of our family with a reputation for threats and violence, not me. No one testified I had ever threatened or attacked anyone.

After the state rested, the judge denied my lawyer's Motions to Direct a Verdict of Acquittal, supposedly due to the confusing facts of the case as presented.

The trial should have ended there. The prosecution had submitted no evidence that I harmed or threatened my sister in any manner.

The only evidence presented by the state against me concerning my mother's death was that she awoke me from sleep and a violent confrontation took place and somehow the rifle she was holding was used to shoot her and got broken; no physical evidence tied that rifle to her or my sister's deaths.

In other words, there was clearly no evidence to support a conviction of first or second-degree murder, the prosecution requested that the jury infer from the surrounding facts and circumstances that I had committed a murder to someone involved. After all, two people were dead; *someone* had to be responsible.

The defense called the state's own medical experts from the Eastern State Hospital, who testified that after extensive testing, in their professional opinion, I had told the truth and really did not know what had happened that fateful night. I had no motive or desire to kill or harm anyone involved.

My defense team then called to the stand Dr. Moorland Prosser, a well known and widely respected forensic psychiatrist from Oklahoma City. The good doctor had flown in during the day to testify and needed to fly back immediately, so everything was rushed. The defense lawyers committed a tactical error when they put the doctor on the stand to testify without him spending any time with me that day.

Dr. Prosser testified that his office tested and interviewed me, and after a review of the state hospital's findings, he determined I was truthful and really had no conscious memory of the events that night.

The doctor was passed to the state, and great harm was done to my position when the doctor was asked, "Did you interview Bobby before you took the stand?"

"No, I did not have time."

"Therefore, doctor, you do not know his current state of mind or his current level of awareness to those events as of today, isn't that correct?"

"Yes, that would be true," replied the doctor.

The state called Jack Stamper, their star rebuttal witness, the publisher of the *Hugo Daily Newspaper* to wrap up their case. After all, Jack had been the only man to get a "full confession" signed by the defendant in this case. It was quite an accomplishment and also quite a big lie and betrayal of a boy's trust.

Jack Stamper had written out his version of a boy killing his mother and sister and burning the family house to cover up the crime. He had even gotten the boy's signature on the supposed confession. Then he printed it boldly in the town's only newspaper.

There was only one slight problem: I never said to Jack Stamper what he wrote. When he showed me what he had written, I used a pen to black out major parts of it out. Jack had not bothered to print the fact that I had marked out any statements of my involvement in the deaths of my mother and sister. He had betrayed my trust and poisoned the community against me.

A noticeable stir occurred in the courtroom and jury box when Jack acknowledged that I had blacked out major portions of the so-called confession given him from my jail cell. Everyone in the courtroom realized the significance of Stamper's admissions. There had been no confessions in this case, only a lot of confusion, contradictions, and outright lying.

The case was a big mess from both viewpoints by this stage of the trial.

Both sides rested and presented their final arguments to a jury that was confused and being asked to try to unravel a mystery.

After many hours of heated debate and deliberations, the jury foreman announced the jury was hopelessly deadlocked by a vote of six to six, and neither side was going to compromise.

The judge granted a mistrial and released the jury and parties.

One male juror was later heard to make the statement, "I do not know what I would do if I woke up to find a rifle in my face—probably the same thing that boy did to save his life."

The news was now out in the community. There had been no confession, and my mother had started whatever happened that night. No one knew what happened to the young innocent girl who died from the blunt force trauma.

The prosecutor's office knew it was now a new ballgame. They had taken their best shot at a defendant who had all the cards stacked against him—public opinion, the press, and all the law enforcement people—and yet they could not get a conviction.

So what did they do next? They filed a felony arson case against me. They assumed it would be like shooting fish in a barrel, a sure thing. I had to post another bail bond for arson; more of a case of sour grapes than a case of arson.

The power of the state is absolute, and woe to those who stand and fight.

———

CHAPTER 28

Trial Two

• • •

THE MISTRIAL WAS A BIG letdown for all concerned, for many reasons. The prosecutor had to get serious about proving his allegations. He had lost his great first advantage of having a jury panel that had already been exposed to all the adverse publicity against me.

The testimony at the first trial was now common knowledge in the community, and many people now questioned the state's position and the accuracy of all the previous newspaper and law enforcement announcements concerning the supposed *confession* of guilt, which no longer seemed accurate.

The county attorney had been out-lawyered, and he knew it and contacted the state attorney general's office to request a crack trial lawyer to assist him in the prosecution of the cases against me in the future.

The mistrial meant my lawyers would have to retry the exhausting case.

The mistrial meant my life remained in a state of limbo, and I still could not join the military and was at the mercy of the state as to when my cases would be reset for jury trial.

One good thing to come of the ordeal was that the cute brunette I had once dated had a ringside seat to the entire trial and had seen the full facts of the case revealed. She realized I was not a monster after all, and we again began dating. I returned to my job in Dallas, and she remained working at the Choctaw County Courthouse in Hugo. We were married shortly thereafter.

My lawyers, Hal Welch and Vester Songer, were convinced the state's case had been weakened considerably, and they were pushing the prosecutor to retry or dismiss it. A new trial date was set for the end of the year, and both sides prepared in earnest, knowing this would probably be the last trial and that one side was going to lose for sure this time.

My lawyers made arrangements with the Oklahoma City psychiatrist, Dr. Prosser, to do further, more vigorous testing of my memory to try to elicit helpful information for the next trial so it would not just be a rerun of the same confusing facts. I needed to be able to take the stand in my own defense and tell the jury what had actually occurred. It was still a blank page to me.

During the summer, I again took several days away from my employer to travel to the doctor's clinic in Oklahoma City for further evaluation and testing of my memory. The doctor put me through the ringer, again. After rigorous written and oral examinations, he admitted me into his hospital, and they prepared me for some type of operation. I was wheeled into a room and injected with an intravenous needle connected to a slow-dripping bottle. The room began to spin, and the next thing I knew, I was trying to count backwards and was in a dreamlike state. I knew someone was asking me questions, but I did not know for sure what my answers were. I finally floated away into another world. When I again realized who I was and where I was, an attendant was standing over my bed.

"What happened to me?" I asked.

"Dr. Prosser administered sodium pentothal to you and then asked you a series of questions. Do you remember?" he asked.

"I vaguely remember him asking me questions, but I do not remember what I said to him," I replied. "Can I leave now?"

"In two hours you will be free to go home."

I was delighted and happily returned to my work and husbandly duties.

My wife and I had rented one unit of a small four-plex apartment in a building shared by three other young couples. Interestingly enough, all of the other three couples were our age, and each of the women was pregnant. My wife soon joined that group to make it unanimous: four young pregnant wives with working husbands.

I did well at Safeway Stores, quickly earning a promotion to a meat department manager at one of their largest volume stores. The district manager for my division of stores remarked I was the best-looking meat department manager they had, and he had me pose for advertising photos that soon appeared in the Dallas newspapers. I held my breath, hoping that no one in Oklahoma bothered to contact the district office of Safeway in Dallas to tell them just how well known I really was in southeastern Oklahoma.

Our beautiful baby girl was born in the fall of 1965. Now my wife could proudly join the four-person baby stroller brigade that proudly marched up and down our streets each day, back and forth to the nearby stores.

Our small family loaded up our car and headed back to Hugo when we received a firm trial date from my lawyers. I took a week's vacation from my job, hoping that would be sufficient time. I knew the last trial had consumed an entire week.

That following Monday morning, everyone appeared at the old courthouse in Hugo, Choctaw County, Oklahoma, to entertain the community again with biggest show in town.

The courthouse was packed with even more jurors this time because of the former difficulty in selecting twelve fair and impartial persons in a community that had been saturated with this story since its beginnings.

The same actors appeared as last time. The only new addition was the tall, loud, and arrogant assistant attorney general and special prosecutor, Jack Swidensky. He was to now lead the prosecution's team.

Folksy old county attorney Jenner would now take a secondary role and try to charm the jury panel. Mr. Jack was no country boy from Oklahoma; his Eastern accent was apparent and irritating to all.

Again it became difficult to select a jury from the panel. Most people had made up their minds already. The one thing that had improved from the defense standpoint was that some of the potential jurors smiled when they looked at me. That had not happened during the previous trial jury selection. The prosecution had to excuse just as many jurors for preconceived notions of my innocence as the defense excused for preconceptions about my guilt.

The atmosphere of the courtroom had changed considerably from the first trial. The lawyers or other participants exchanged no pleasantries. Everyone knew this was the final show.

After both parties declared, "Ready for trial," to presiding Judge Philips, my lawyer, Hal Welch, announced to the court that the defense had a special issue to try before the jury first before the murder cases would be tried.

Special Prosecutor Swidensky exploded with objections, which the court listened to and overruled.

The defense wanted a jury finding on whether or not I had in fact suffered from amnesia on the occasion in question, because if I had, then the state had no evidence of my guilt, because by the state's own admission, the only evidence they had against me were my own so-called statements and admissions.

An audible groan arose from the county attorney. He had been out-lawyered again, and the murder cases were now in danger of falling apart altogether if my statements were excluded.

The burden of proof rested on my lawyers and me to prove the existence of my amnesia. The prosecutor only needed to attack our evidence and try to sway the jury to vote against the special issue of the existence of amnesia.

The state's entire case would evaporate if my statements could not be used against me in court.

Dr. Prosser had flown in earlier that day to interview me in detail. My lawyers were not going to make that mistake again. Dr. Prosser took the stand and testified at length to the exhaustive testing done by the doctors of psychology and psychiatry at Eastern State Hospital and at his clinic. In the doctor's professional opinion, I had complete amnesia of the events surrounding my mother and sister's deaths.

He explained that the human mind is a complex and fragile mechanism and that I was a victim of dissociative psychogenic amnesia, which is caused as a result of overwhelming stress or traumatic events that a person has experienced or witnessed.

"The mind has the ability to suppress or block a person's ability to retrieve certain events in their lives. This type of amnesia is often seen in cases of sexual abuse of children or in combat where the person's mind cannot consciously understand or mentally process what is happening to them or around them. That part of their memory is just not there for them to retrieve. Sudden onset amnesia can follow a traumatic event in a person's life that is life-threatening, such as Bobby has explained from what he remembers."

On cross-examination, Jack, the prosecutor, walked into a buzz saw that he soon regretted. "How do you know for sure Bobby is not just faking to save his hide? Did you give him truth serum?"

"Yes, we did. Bobby was administered sodium pentothal under closely monitored hospital procedures a few months ago, and he was questioned."

I could hear the court attorney's heavy breathing over the thick silence of the courtroom. Everyone had always wondered about this testimony. *How do you know an amnesia victim is telling the truth?* This testimony would determine the outcome of this trial, and everyone in the courtroom knew it.

Dr. Prosser continued talking as Jack tried to recover from his clumsy cross-examination.

"Diagnosis of traumatic amnesia is difficult. The first thing we do is test for organic brain injury. There was none found in Bobby's case. Then we experts try extensive psychotherapy, or talk therapy: talking to the patient to try to find the causes and triggers to the suppressed memories. Usually that type of therapy will solve the problem. It did not in Bobby's case. We then moved on to the use of chemicals to try to release those depressed memories. We administered sufficient amounts of sodium pentothal to Bobby to convince ourselves he was being truthful and was not faking his symptoms."

Jack continued his losing battle. "So how does the sodium pentothal detect frauds?"

"The central nervous system is depressed, and inhibitory neurons, which normally assist in falsehoods, are depressed; concentration and wakefulness is depressed, and the patient starts a free-flowing expression of his feelings, thoughts, and reactions, and will truthfully answer questions when questioned."

Prosecutor Jack passed the witness before he did any more harm to the state's case.

County Attorney Jenner then asked Dr. Prosser if he had talked to and interviewed me that day before the doctor began testifying.

"Yes, I did interview Bobby at length this morning, and his memory of those events is still completely blocked and unavailable to assist in his defense."

That was the end of Dr. Prosser's testimony, and he was excused to fly back to Oklahoma City.

Lawyer Welch then called a surprise witness, and the courtroom went suddenly silent. The prosecutors exchanged worried looks.

My attorney called Sheriff Thornton to the stand, and even I was surprised and a little alarmed. I had never spoken with the sheriff concerning any of the events in my case. But he had done great harm to me when he had given statements that were published in most of the local newspapers and in the major publications in the state, including the *Daily Oklahoman*.

The sheriff, who had never questioned me or even spoken to me, had stated to the press that we had the following exchange:

"Was your mother shot with your rifle?"

"Yes."

"Was your sister hit over the head with your rifle?"

"Yes."

"Did you do it?"

"I need my lawyer." (That was strange, since I did not have a lawyer then.)

Sheriff Thorton had also stated to the press, "Wilson admits he poured gasoline all over the house and lit a match to it."

So why was my lawyer calling a man who had done his best to convict me in the press?

The short, portly sheriff, in full uniform, took the stand. The courtroom was now standing room only and deathly quiet.

"What is your name and occupation?" Hal questioned.

"I am Ed Thornton, sheriff of Choctaw County, Oklahoma."

"Were you acting sheriff of this county back in June, 1963?"

"Yes, sir."

"Did you learn about the deaths of Lavonne and Judy Wilson from your officers?"

"Yes, I did."

"Did your office investigate those deaths?"

"Yes, they did."

"Do you recognize Bobby Wilson seated here next to me?"

"Yes, I do. Seen him many times last couple of years."

"Was he in your county jail for eight months following his arrest?"

"Yes, he was."

"Have you ever interviewed him about the deaths of his mother and sister?"

"No, I have not."

"Have you ever asked Bobby how his mother and sister died or why their house burned?"

"No, I have not."

"Have you ever personally heard Bobby Wilson ever tell anyone he killed his mother and sister and burned their house?"

"No, I have not."

"So if anyone has ever quoted you as saying any of those things about Bobby here, they would either be mistaken or just outright lying. Is that true?"

"Yes, that would be true. As far as I personally know, Bobby Wilson never told anyone he killed his mother and sister, and the only thing he said about the fire from what I have heard discussed is that he was the only person left alive in the house before the fire started."

"Thank you, Sheriff. Pass the witness."

The prosecutors were too stunned to ask the sheriff anything. Many faces turned to watch the sheriff leave the courtroom.

The state's case was coming apart at the seams. It was built on lies and deceitful press reports, and the chickens were coming home to roost.

My lawyers rested their case, and the state called their star witness, Jack Stamper, local newspaper publisher, to the stand. He recounted his story of the signed and printed newspaper confession I had supposedly given to him.

On cross-examination, he had to admit he had neglected to mention to the public I had crossed out any self-incriminating parts of the so-called signed confession. The entire document, with the crossed out portions, was admitted as evidence to let the jurors examine it themselves and make their own decision.

Both parties rested their cases and presented their closing arguments to the jury.

The jury was only in deliberations for a few hours this time and returned a verdict in my favor, finding that I did in fact have amnesia of the events in question.

The verdict effectively rendered useless to the prosecution any statements I had made concerning the events in question. The state dismissed their arson case against me and took the entire matter under advisement until further notice. No further trial dates were mentioned or discussed.

Everyone was emotionally drained after the jury returned the verdict. I asked my lawyers what I could expect in the future. I still wanted to join the military, and I was twenty-one years old now.

"Just take it a day at a time," Hal said. "Go on with your life like nothing happened and try to move forward and do not look back. I doubt the state wants to go to trial again."

I loaded up my wife and baby, drove back to Dallas, and returned to work Monday morning like nothing unusual had happened in my life while I was away on *vacation*.

I found out months later why the sheriff had changed his spots. It seems that letter I wrote to my father while locked in jail, which my cellmate James had slipped in the mail, had been returned with the notation "moved, left no address" to the county jail and the sheriff had opened it and read its contents. In it, I outlined in detail my life since my father had walked out of our lives. The sheriff then decided to set the record straight about me, and what he really knew about my case. He had previously stood by while a great injustice was done, and he wanted to make things right while he still could. After a lot of soul searching, he decided he needed to make the truth public before he left office.

I always wondered what he would have done if I had been convicted at the first trial.

CHAPTER 29

Work and School

• • •

OVER THE NEXT SIX MONTHS, I focused my thoughts and energy on my job and family. I was still in a legal limbo with no end in sight, but now I had a wife and baby girl who depended on me, and I wanted them to have a happy home.

The work I did for Safeway Stores was mentally and physically exhausting, and at the end of the day, I was content to play with my daughter and watch television or go to an occasional drive-in movie. Our one experiment with hiring a baby-sitter turned out badly when we returned home to find our daughter with a busted mouth and lip that required a trip to the emergency room. Thereafter, we just went to the drive-in movies with the baby and warmed her milk bottle on the hot car's engine manifold.

The Safeway district manager had his eye on me for future promotions and mentioned to me that I should try to take advantage of the college tuition reimbursement program my employer offered to its full-time employees. The program only required an employee to make a grade of C or better on courses at an accredited college, and Safeway would reimburse the employee for his college tuition: fees, books, and supplies not included.

By the date of my twenty-second birthday in September, I was ready to start college. I talked to my wife, and she agreed to the sacrifices necessary. I would be going to work earlier in the mornings, while she and the baby were still asleep. After work, I would drive directly to the college campus and attend classes until ten o'clock at night, Monday through Thursday nights, and I would not arrive back home until about eleven o'clock on those nights, after everyone had gone to bed.

She and our baby would probably not even see me those four days a week. Basically, our social life would cease, at least as far as my participation was concerned, because I would be need to study at each and every opportunity, even on my days off from work.

Luckily, my wife had several lady friends, who each had a young baby and husbands who were also attending college classes at night, so she could socialize with them.

Going back to school, especially to college, was a shock to me after being away from studying for more than three years. I had forgotten all the math and English I had learned in high school. My first college grades were poor, and I needed help. But with my demanding work and school schedule, I had no way to make time for tutoring. So I stopped at a nearby public library and checked out old high school math and English textbooks and taught myself everything I had forgotten since my high school graduation.

My grades improved, and my mind and body adapted to my new work/study routine.

I started college in September, on my twenty-second birthday. I started taking six college hours per semester and was soon taking up to nine college hours per semester, year round, including the summer sessions. I was able to accumulate approximately thirty college hours per year with this rigorous schedule of classes, all at night.

I was working full-time during the day and going to college four nights per week.

By the time my twenty-fourth birthday arrived, I had ninety hours of college completed at the University of Texas at Arlington, Texas campus. I needed thirty more college hours to graduate with a degree, but those classes were only conducted during the day and not at night.

This change meant my income was going to drop considerably since I would be working only on the weekends and going to college during the day for the entire week.

My wife and I went on a tight budget so we could keep our expenses low and still have adequate funds to provide necessities of life for our growing daughter and us.

Working each weekend and going to college each weekday was a fairly brutal schedule, but I committed myself to finishing my college degree.

Nothing seemed to happen with the criminal cases pending in Oklahoma; they seemed to have faded into the past. Each time our telephone rang at home, I expected to receive a call to load up and get ready for another trial. The call never came.

It was now 1970, and almost seven years had passed with no final decision by the Choctaw County Attorney concerning the criminal cases hanging over my head like the proverbial axe.

It shocked and saddened me to learn of the unexpected death of my lead defense attorney, Hal Welch. I had always felt confident and secure that he would protect my legal rights to freedom as long as he was alive. With his passing, I suddenly felt alone again, insecure and vulnerable to the state's steamrollers. I spent many restless nights wondering what to do about my future. I was unsure what the future held for my family and I, and I knew there was the possibility one day I would receive that phone call to get ready for trial one more time.

I finally decided to go to law school and become a lawyer myself; then I would know what steps to take to defend others and myself caught up in similar circumstances.

I spoke with my wife about it, and she was disappointed to learn that three more years of sacrifice and budgeting were in our future.

Our friends, each with a young child, like ourselves, were looking forward to settling down and buying new homes, furniture, and automobiles as soon as the husbands graduated from college.

I decided to talk to my college counselor about my thoughts of going forward and obtaining a law school education.

I met with him, and he discouraged me with the words, "You are almost twenty-five years old. You have a family to support and limited resources. It is too high a hill to climb at your age. You should stay with your employer since you now have seven years of your time invested with them."

I took the counselor's advice as a challenge and later told my wife I intended to apply for admission at the leading law school in Texas, based on the state's bar exam pass-fail ratio scores. That law school had a freshman class limited to only about 150 entering students at that time, so securing entrance was certainly going to be a challenge.

I was in my senior year at the University of Texas at Arlington, and while my grades were well above average, a student really needed almost an A average to have any hope of gaining entrance to one of the state's leading schools of law.

I decided to become politically active on campus and entered the race for president of the campus political and pre-law fraternity. I won that election by one vote.

I had read of a political feud between several of the deans of the state's leading law schools. It seemed to be personal, and several preeminent law schools had declined to invite the dean of the law school I wanted to attend to join their good ol' boys social gatherings

Seizing on this pubic snubbing of the new dean, I invited him to our university to address all the pre-law and political science majors at our upcoming annual meeting, and I declined to invite any other law school deans in the state. The invited dean graciously accepted, and I picked him up at Love Field Airport in my car and drove him back later after his speech.

When I drove him back to the airport, I complimented him on his speech delivery and informed him I was only going to apply at his law school for admission since it was the only one in the state of Texas I was willing to attend. He looked at me and then wrote my name down in his notebook. I filled out my application for his school that week and was soon accepted for admission that upcoming fall.

I was entering a new stage in my life. I was probably the only man who ever enrolled in law school with murder charges pending.

At least I already had firsthand knowledge of the American criminal justice system, seen from the inside, unlike the other law students, who were on the outside looking in. They would be looking in without a clue about how the real world of criminal justice was administered to the weak and helpless in America.

———

CHAPTER 30
Learning Law

• • •

THE FIRST YEAR OF LAW school completely immerses the student in the topics of property, contract, and tort law, which represent the three great areas of the civil law. Surprisingly, criminal law is treated like a stepchild in law school. Most law professors treat the subject with disdain. It is as if any law student who wants to specialize in criminal law and procedure is probably just going to be an outcast lawyer and probably a drunkard anyway, so why bother with them and *their kind*. Of course, the law faculty also feels the same way about their C grade students, and those students are the ones who make all the money practicing law, and the law schools are constantly asking them for donations.

The criminal law and procedure classes were elective classes and not even required for a student to graduate.

It soon became apparent to me that the first year of law school was just an endurance contest to see who could stand the stress and strain on their minds.

The amount of assigned reading each day was impossible and mind-boggling. The students who took the professor's assigned reading literally were soon overwhelmed and started dropping out of school very quietly. One day a student who sat next to you in class would just disappear, not to be seen again.

The professors took great delight in calling on the individual students to stand up in front of the class and humiliating them with legal questions that even a seasoned lawyer could not answer intelligently. At least that taught us to think fast and on our feet.

There was only one exam given for each of the major courses, which were almost ten months long. Whatever grade the student received on that one exam determined his or her final grade in that class for the year. You had to maintain a grade average of seventy or above to remain in school for the second or third years. It was the movie *Paper Chase* in real time.

Needless to say, approximately thirty-five percent of the freshman class was gone by the end of the final exams the first year.

In order to keep food on the table and have a decent place to live, I had to work each weekend while in law school, a practice the law school administration greatly discouraged. After all, they wanted the student's entire life focused on studying law books and nothing else, because supposedly nothing was more important in a student's life except studying the law. Actually, my financial need to do physical work each weekend was a life-saver, because by the end of each week of freshman law studies, each student was stressed to the breaking point and needed some type of physical exercise to release all the built up stress.

The freshman class was divided into three sections, A, B, and C. These three sections soon morphed into baseball teams, who met in combat each Saturday afternoon and played baseball with great abandon, vigor, and beer drinking. One student even died of a stroke during one particularly grueling game.

We enrolled my daughter in a private pre-school and kindergarten during my law school experience.

She joined me at our home study desk each night while I studied law books into the early morning hours. She brought her coloring and early reading books and worked alongside me until she fell asleep, and I would carry her to her bed.

Her early study habits would pay off in the future, when she was always the top student in her classes.

I made it through the first year of law school with fairly good grades and began the second year taking all the criminal evidence and procedure courses I was allowed. It was then that I studied in-depth the major Warren Supreme Court decisions that had recently become the law of the land, cases such as *In Re Gault* (1967) in which the court ruled that juveniles charged with criminal offenses are entitled to due process of law, including right to legal counsel and self-incrimination warnings.

In *Miranda v. Arizona* (1966), the court ruled that arrest suspects must be warned in advance of their right to remain silent and to have an attorney appointed. Those were much needed changes in our justice system. I was living proof of that.

I listened as the professor bantered with the class full of students about whether such Constitutional protections were really needed in our society. "After all, aren't the law enforcement personnel just trying to protect the public from criminals?" he asked.

I knew firsthand why such protections were needed. They were needed for the innocent, the poor, and the non-professional criminal suspects who were occasionally caught up in a police investigation. I knew the professional crooks and career criminals knew better than open their mouths during police interrogations.

The Supreme Court rulings were meant to protect the innocents and the unwary that their own words could be used against them or possibly twisted later to create some type of confession or admission against their own interest.

By the end of my second year of law school, I had trained my mind to look for the legal issues the professors took great delight in concealing in their elaborate essay exams. The trick to making a good grade in the law classes was developing the ability to spot those hidden legal issues, buried within complicated situations. I did well on my second year exams. I had discovered the secret to good grades in law school and on the state bar exam.

When I finished my second year, I began getting restless to try my hand at the actual practice of law. Law school was becoming a great bore to me and also to most of my classmates.

That summer, I found an intern position open at a local law firm and began working on real criminal cases instead of the theoretical kind thrown around in class each day, ad nauseam.

The law firm I interned with was required to do some *pro bono* legal work to please the Bar Association. The firm usually assigned its law school interns to do the grunt work on these cases. That was me. The two cases assigned to me were pretty hopeless looking at first glance.

One case involved an undocumented Mexican farmhand who was nineteen and charged with first-degree murder. Three witnesses had seen him walk up behind another teenage Mexican illegal and hit him with a double-bladed chopping axe, neatly decapitating him. The defendant gave no reason for his actions. The dead boy had been writing a letter to his mother when he was slain. I could not think of a more hopeless set of facts to work with.

I located a bilingual college student, and we drove out to the scene of the homicide. The three witnesses to the killing all worked for the farmer, as did the defendant and the deceased. All five shared a mobile home provided by the farmer.

I talked to the farmer, and he said the defendant was a hardworking fellow who never gave anyone any problems. He was honest and a good kid. The dead boy was somewhat of a prima donna and avoided hard work as much as possible. He usually just stayed at the mobile home and kept house and did the cooking and washing for the other four young workers.

I began to suspect there was more going on in the mobile home shared by these workers than was apparent to the casual observer. I also observed that all of the workers were Catholics.

I asked the farmer if there was a Catholic priest in the area, and he informed me where the workers occasionally went to Mass on Sundays.

I contacted the priest of the church and asked him to accompany me to the county jail to speak with our client, the defendant. He was glad to assist me and had only good things to say about the accused young man. He was concerned about what could have caused such a brutal act.

The Catholic priest was semi-retired and only worked occasionally. He was bilingual, which was important, since the defendant was very poor with his English, and I was very poor with Spanish.

At first, the accused only looked down at the floor and refused to discuss the matter with us. I had the priest explain to the accused how important it was for us to know if he had reason to attack the dead boy. I directed the priest to ask the accused why the dead boy did all the cooking and cleaning for the other four workers. I watched the boy's eyes flash at this question, and he looked at me with fear in his eyes. My suspicions were correct. The Mexican *macho* factor was in play.

I asked the priest to ask the boy if the dead boy was homosexual. The priest hesitated for a moment, looking at me with great concern in his eyes. Then he turned to the boy, whose reaction to the question removed any doubt from my mind.

The boy then broke down tearfully and told us what had occurred that day. The dead boy had made repeated sexual advances toward the accused at night, when the other workers were asleep. The accused even locked himself in the closet at night on several occasions to avoid the advances. He was very much afraid *he* would be labeled as a homosexual if the other workers discovered anything sexual occurring between the two of them. He had warned the dead boy that the next time he made advances; he would be met with violence.

On the day in question, the accused awoke from a nap to find an open letter lying on his chest in which the dead boy professed his romantic love. The defendant's reaction was the violent attack on the deceased.

I obtained an affidavit from the priest as to the defendant's story, and the lawyer handling the boy's case was able to negotiate a plea deal with the local prosecutor for a five-year term for manslaughter. The murder case was dropped. The defendant received credit for the seven months he spent in jail awaiting trial. The client was very grateful, as were his parents, for the final outcome.

The other case assigned to me was that of a middle-aged Negro man who supposedly had hit and seriously injured his wife in a domestic dispute. Our client said the wife attacked him with a butcher knife and he was just defending himself. The police did not believe him, and he was charged with attempted murder. No knife had been found around the wife's body before she was taken to the hospital by ambulance. She denied having a knife.

I talked to the client in jail, and he swore that his wife came out of their kitchen, running at him with a butcher knife, and he had hit her for protection only, with no intent to harm her.

Again, the facts looked pretty bleak. My lawyer boss subpoenaed all the state's evidence for inspection and sent me to look through the box full of photos and physical evidence taken by the crime scene crew and police.

There must have been fifty large photographs taken of the interior of the house and each room therein. I painstakingly looked at the items one by one, looking for anything that might assist in our client's defense. The confrontation between the couple had taken place in the middle of their living room. I looked at all the photos from all possible angles, and then something caught my eye.

In one photo I saw what appeared to be a knife handle lying on the TV stand in the living room. But other photos of the living room and TV stand showed no knife handle. Someone had removed the knife during the crime scene investigation. It could have been moved accidentally or on purpose, but it had disappeared. I made a photocopy of this photo and finished my examination. That photocopy alone was sufficient to have the charge reduced to simple assault and the client released with credit for four months already served in the county jail. He was very pleased.

The law firm was impressed with my efforts, and when my third year of law school started, they offered me a part-time job of twenty hours per week. That was fine with me, and I stopped working on the weekends in the grocery business and worked four hours per day in the afternoon for the law firm.

On the weekends, I started studying for the state bar exam. At that time in Texas, a person could take the state bar exam if he had completed sixty hours of law school. That made me eligible to take the bar exam that following January, even though I would not officially graduate until the end of May. Only a few law students from my school were brash enough to think they could pass the bar exam before they even finished law school.

The four-day bar exam was grueling and exhausting, but I passed with one of the highest grades and was sworn in as a licensed lawyer in April, two months before graduation from law school.

After graduation, I had to decide what I wanted to do with my new legal career. The firm where I worked offered me a permanent position, but I graciously declined and wanted to return to the more familiar Dallas area.

I interviewed with Joe Tonahill, a famous lawyer from Jasper, Texas, who had been one of Jack Ruby's lawyers, and he offered me a job. But Jasper did not seem to be my kind of town.

I had worked in Senator Ralph Yarborough's reelection campaign at one time, and his brother, a well-known

Dallas injury lawyer, offered me a position, but injury law did not appeal to me.

I drove around the county seats near Dallas until I saw an old courthouse that caught my interest. I was walking around inside the old three-story courthouse when an older gentleman asked if he could assist me. "No thanks, I was just admiring your courthouse," I replied. He introduced himself as the local county judge. I told him I had just finished law school and been licensed and was looking around the Dallas area for some likely towns to open a law office.

The old gentlemen smiled broadly. He shook my hand again, held on, pulled me into his nearby office, and offered me a chair.

"This town desperately needs some new legal talent. Please open an office here, and I will personally see that you have all the legal work you can handle," he offered.

He was so persuasive, I could not say no. He even located a vacant office site for me and called the owner, another local attorney.

I drove home and told my wife and daughter, "We are moving to a new town, a new house, and a new life."

They were delighted to know I had finally located a town to settle down in and enjoy the American Dream, at least for a while.

———

CHAPTER 31
Shock and Awe

• • •

TRUE TO HIS WORD, THE old county judge started assigning me as court appointed attorney for many of his unrepresented juveniles. I took an almost daily trip to the county courthouse to appear in his juvenile court and then walk over to the county jail, where the juveniles were initially kept until usually being released to their parents until their formal adjudication hearings. These frequent trips allowed me to get very familiar with the courthouse and county jail personnel.

One afternoon, after an appearance in the juvenile court, I decided to walk next door and talk to the assistant county attorney to discuss a certain juvenile case with the prosecutor.

When I walked into his office, I noticed loud talking coming from an adjacent conference interrogation room. The door was open, and I walked over and looked in on an obvious police interrogation going on between two burly, middle-aged, white police detectives and a very distraught young Negro woman, who was trying to talk and cry at the same time. I had no idea who any of the actors were or what the obviously distressing and heated conversation was about.

"Tell us why you shot your boyfriend," one detective was almost shouting in her ear on one side. The other detective was standing behind her, leaning over her, and talking in her other ear. "Was he pimping for you?" he demanded. "Was it over money you owed him?"

The small woman sat in a folding chair with her face in her hands, shaking her head. She was obviously very distraught and confused.

The detectives noticed my presence in the doorway, and one of them walked over to the door, and without a word to me, closed the door loudly to show his displeasure with my interest.

I walked over to the young lady receptionist for the prosecutor's office and asked her, "What's going on?" I pointed toward the closed door.

"She shot her boyfriend at a rural service station early this morning, and they want to get a confession out of her before anyone else talks to her. I feel sorry for her; she seems really upset and keeps asking to call her mother about her baby."

"Why is she so concerned about her baby?" I said. "She better get herself a lawyer but quick. Has anyone been checking on her?"

"No, she doesn't even live around here. She is from Oklahoma City and says she left her baby alone in her apartment. She says she and her boyfriend stopped for gas, had an argument, and he was shot to death. That is all I know."

The receptionist shrugged and went back to typing and chewing her gum.

The assistant county attorney had gone home for the day, so I walked out the courthouse door and down the steps to my parked car and sat there for a while, staring off in space, thinking. That scene I had just witnessed in the interrogation room bothered me a great deal. The young woman was about the same age I had been when I was arrested, and I was quite shaken by the feelings I was having. She was obviously quite upset and stressed by the events of this morning and in no mental condition to be questioned in such a confrontational manner. And she had no family and no lawyer to help or protect her rights. She was easy prey for some overzealous cops who just wanted to quickly wrap things up in a neat little bundle with a full confession.

I drove over to the county jail and asked the jailer if the woman had been able to call any of her family when she had been booked into the jail. He laughed and said, "No, she didn't have any change to use the pay phone to call her mother, and no one would loan her any. She kept hollering that her baby was alone in her apartment in Oklahoma City, and no one even knew where she was. She does not appear to have any family, but she shot the shit out of her boyfriend. The detectives think he was her pimp. She had no money on her, and the car was registered to her."

I drove back to the courthouse; this case really started to bother me. Most lawyers would have just walked away. But these facts were too near and dear to me for comfort. My pulse was fast and my breathing heavy as I walked quickly back to the courthouse and bounded up the stone steps to the second floor county attorney's office. I walked past the surprised receptionist without a word and opened the interrogation room door, and the two detectives quickly confronted me. "What do you think you are doing?" One of them was in my face with his hand on his gun.

"I am her lawyer, so leave her alone. No more interrogation. It stops now!" I was in his face now.

Both detectives backed up, and their faces fell almost to the floor. The party was over.

I turned to face the wide-eyed and surprised girl, her face and blouse now wet from tears and sweat. "I am your lawyer; I just got off the phone with your brother. He is on his way here from Oklahoma City, and he hired me to represent you. You make no further statements to anyone unless I am present, understand?" She nodded her head, still staring at me in amazement.

I handed her my business card and four quarters and told her, "Only call me and your mother, and only talk to me about your case, understand?"

"Yes, sir!" was her quick and weak reply.

I walked out of the room to the receptionist's desk and told her, "Have the county court bailiff take my client back to the jail while I make arrangements for a bail bond to be set on her case."

I walked out of the courthouse and back to my vehicle. I was shaking like a leaf. I had probably violated several provisions of State Bar Canon of Ethics, but I really did not care at that moment. If I was going to be a lawyer, I was not going to allow anyone within my view to be abused by the legal system like I had been years earlier. I could already tell being a criminal defense lawyer with my background was going to be a constant battle between *the system* and my own experiences with the system.

I did not sleep well that night; in fact, I did not sleep at all. I walked the floor in our living room and dining room at four o'clock in the morning like I used to walk the floor of that old jail bullpen in the early morning hours, driving the jailer below me slowly crazy. It was poetic justice, because he never knew who it was walking that jailhouse floor like a caged animal at four and five o'clock in the morning. But I owed him, and it was a debt that needed paying, in spades.

I could not put my finger on why I reacted so personally to this black woman's situation. Race had nothing to do with it. It was the imagery of her case that had affected me so strongly; I could see the look of hopelessness and despair in her face.

I had once been there, and it was not a pleasant place to visit. I knew she would break down and quickly become cannon fodder for the justice system unless someone acted quickly. She would soon say anything they wanted her to say.

The detectives would come up with their own version of what they thought *should have occurred* and would announce to the public how another crazed killer was behind bars and everyone could sleep better due to quick and decisive action by the crack investigating team.

I was not in the mood to spend the day in my law office that morning dealing with clients and their problems. I told my secretary I needed to work on a new murder case and would be out all day.

"What new murder case?" she asked as I walked out of my office's front door.

I had a legal pad and my camera and drove to the county jail to interview my new client. She was brought down to the conference room, and the jailer informed me that she had been charged with capital murder, her car had been impounded as evidence, and the magistrate said it was a no bail bond case.

That was certainly not encouraging news, but not unexpected. The state always tries to render the helpless even more helpless so they will just surrender themselves to the higher power of the state. Take everything and leave them with nothing: no assets, no friends, and no hope.

My new client smiled weakly and extended her hand. "I don't know why you did what you did or why you are helping me, but God bless you." Her voice started to crack.

I took her hand and held it. I looked into her brown eyes and told her, "I do not want to see you abused. If you want, I will call your mother for you and step out of the picture, and you can hire a lawyer of your choice."

I released her hand. She smiled and said, "I do not have a brother, but you will do fine as my lawyer. But I have no money to pay you with. My car was the only thing I owned. I was able to call my mother last night with your quarters, and she went to get my baby boy, and he is fine now. Thank you. You saved his life."

"Well, if you still want me to be your lawyer, tell me what happened to you yesterday morning. Anything you tell me is confidential and will not be used against you," I said and started taking notes.

"The dead man was my old boyfriend and the father of my year-old baby. I am nineteen years old. I broke up with my boyfriend several weeks ago and threw him out of my apartment in Oklahoma City. He was twenty-three and a thief. I found stolen property in my car trunk, which he had stolen from a house, and I made him pack and leave. He came over the other night to try to talk me into taking him back. We talked and argued until after midnight, and I finally got mad and told him to leave. He said he would leave peacefully and not bother me anymore if I would come down to my car and drive him to the bus station so he could leave town. My baby was asleep in his bed, and it was only a few blocks to the bus station, so I agreed to loan him twenty dollars for a bus ticket, which was all the money I had. We walked down to my car, and he said he had some stuff hidden under my back seat that he needed to get and take with him.

"He pulled up the rear seat and reached down and came up with a sawed-off 12-gauge shotgun. He grabbed me by my hair with his other hand and threw me into the back seat and stuck the barrel of the shotgun in my face. He told me to shut up and not say a word and rolled me over and tied my hands behind my back with his belt. Then he got in the front seat, and we started driving south. He said we were going to Mexico, and I was going to be his whore. He was going to sell my sweet ass to a Mexican who had money. He said he had *connections* across the border from Laredo, Texas, who would help him out and pay a few hundred dollars to buy me for his stable of girls.

"I cried and begged him to just let me out of the car because there was no one to care for my baby. I would just walk back, and he could keep the car, and I would not even call the police on him because he was the baby's father.

"He just told me to shut up and get some rest, because we would be driving for two days. He turned up the radio loud to drown out my screaming at him and crying. I started trying to get my hands untied. We drove for hours and drove through Dallas and kept going south on the interstate. It was just breaking dawn when he noticed we were running out of gas. He stopped the car and took all my change and credit cards from my purse, and we just made it to an all-night, self-serve gas station. He had to get out of the car to pump the gas and pay for it. I saw a chance to escape.

"I was faking being asleep in the backseat. I had worked my hands out of the belt without him noticing. He could not walk over to pay the gas attendant while carrying a gun, so he looked in the back seat, thought I was asleep, stuck that gun under the front seat, and went to pay for the gas.

"As soon as he was gone, I jumped out and reached under the front seat. I grabbed the shotgun and was walking away from the car. He saw me and came running over to stop me. I stopped, raised the gun, pointed it at him, and told him to get away from me and take the car and go, just leave me alone.

"He kept coming toward me, and I screamed, 'Come any closer and I will shoot you.' He kept coming, and I backed up until I was against my car. He reached for the gun barrel and jerked it toward himself, and both barrels went off, hitting him. He spun around and fell across the hood of my car. Blood was everywhere. I screamed and screamed for I don't know how long until an ambulance attendant put me in restraints. Next thing I remember, I was in that interview room with those two detectives for hours. They said my boyfriend was my pimp and I was his whore, and we had a fight about money, and I shot him in cold blood. They said I needed to have a "come to Jesus meeting" with them and come clean and get it off my chest so I could get back to my baby. That is when you came in and everything stopped. I would have said anything to get them to leave me alone and to get someone to take care of my baby."

I laid down my legal pad and looked her in the eyes.

"So why did they think he was your pimp?" I asked.

"They ran a criminal check on him, and he had an arrest record for procuring, which, you know, is a legal term for pimping," she said.

"Yes, I know. I worked on such cases while I was in law school."

"How long have you been lawyer? You seem pretty young to be a lawyer," she asked.

"Oh, about six months. Is that a problem?" I inquired with a smile.

"No, you are the best lawyer I ever met," she replied with a twinkle in her eye.

"And how many lawyers have you ever met?"

"None."

"Okay, you need to keep in mind at all times what I told you. Do not discuss your case with anyone but me—no relatives, no trustees, no inmates, no cops, no anybody. Understand?"

"You are the boss; my life and my baby's life are in your hands." She smiled and shook my hand.

"I am going out to the scene of the shooting. Did anyone actually see you shoot your old boyfriend?" I asked.

"For an instant I saw a woman's face in a passing vehicle. She jammed on her brakes and covered her face with both hands and turned away. She did not stop, and no one else saw it as far as I know. The station attendant's view was completely blocked, they said."

"Did you tell the cops that a woman saw the shooting?"

"Yes, but they said there was no way of locating her, and they disregarded it."

I drove directly to the service station location she described. I had often stopped there myself because it was on the local state highway to Dallas and also at the state highway intersection with the interstate highway to South Texas. It would have been the route someone would take traveling from Oklahoma City to Laredo, Texas. The station was one of those twenty-four hour self-service gasoline only stations with one cashier locked inside a secure small building with a money tray that was slid in and out for payments. It was located about twenty miles from the county courthouse in an isolated rural area with no other houses or buildings around.

When I arrived at the location, it was still roped off with police tape, and a single vehicle was parked at one gasoline pump. Blood covered the front hood. No one was there, and the cashier booth was closed. I took my camera and started taking photos of the scene. I walked over to the old sedan and bent down to examine the blood spatter closely, which was very heavy and very dark, almost black. I was suddenly overcome with dizziness, dropped my camera, and grabbed the car bumper with both hands for support. There was an odor I had smelled before, and I found myself sitting on the ground, leaning against the car's front wheel for support. My mind started to race. Smelling *that odor* again had suddenly released the full memory of what had happened to me that fateful morning back on June 19, 1963. That was the same odor that I had struggled so mightily to recognize that morning and which I could not get my mind wrapped around. And, ten years later, seemingly out of nowhere, it all came crashing down in my mind. *That odor* was the smell of large amounts of blood and gasoline mixed together.

That is what I had smelled that morning, a mix of blood and gasoline. It was the only thing I had truly and clearly remembered, *that odor*. I could never understand what created it or what it was I smelled that morning. Now I knew, and I knew it all.

All my repressed memories of my mother's and sister's deaths came flooding into my conscious mind for the first time, and a great relief came over me.

For the first time, I consciously realized what had happened to my family and how the house was burned, and I also knew for the first time that I had not been responsible for what happened. I was no more guilty of murder than this young lady was. What had happened to her and me could have happened to anyone who was just trying to live a decent life and was caught up in a nightmare of events not of their making.

I sweated profusely and pulled myself up, using the car for support. And, sure enough, I could see the gasoline stains on the ground where I stood, where people had often overfilled their car tanks and it spilled onto this spot. An even darker stain of human blood covered the gasoline stain. This man had bled out all his life's blood on that very spot. Here I stood, overcome by that odor and my own history of death.

I knew now that a higher authority had directed me to help that woman. It was also time for me to come to terms with my own experience in Dante's inferno. I could tell the world what had happened to me in those predawn hours ten years earlier. But with the passage of ten years, I wondered if anyone even cared about the truth anymore. Everyone had moved on with their lives, including me.

I finished taking my photos of the vehicle and the area, and drove back to my office to come up with a defense for my new client. The physical facts at the scene seemed to verify what she had told me. But I would need more proof that she was in fear of her life and that the ex-boyfriend's death was either self-defense or an accident. I needed more than just her testimony.

I got back to my office after closing time, and my secretary had left. That was good, because I could pace back and forth on my office floor and also do some legal research.

Since no bond was going to be set in this case, my client was probably looking at many months of sitting alone in her jail cell, awaiting trial, like I had.

One legal way to short circuit the criminal justice system was to demand the prosecutor immediately prove his case in an examining trial. The state must prove a prima-facie case. No defense lawyer, in his or her right mind would usually pull such a stunt because it was a good way to piss off the prosecutor and the judge, who only wanted to try a criminal case once, not twice.

But I did not care if I gave the local district attorney or judge indigestion if it meant this young woman was not going to be kept away from her baby for maybe a year while she rotted in jail.

I dictated a Demand for an Examining Trial for my secretary to type in the morning. I would file it by noon, and the examining trial had to be held within a few days or the law required the defendant to be released. I would soon be labeled Night Court Bob by the local district attorney for making him and his staff work at night. It was not meant as a compliment.

I still needed to locate a witness for this shooting to verify my client's version of the events. I sat down in my office chair and turned on the most effective tool I had at my disposal: my imagination. Only the great lawyers use that legal tool to its full extent.

I pictured my client backed against her vehicle at about five o'clock in the morning, just breaking daylight. A woman drove by. Who was she and where was she going? I remembered a large steel mill located about a mile away. No woman goes to work at a steel mill at five o'clock in the morning. But wait—what if she is picking up her husband or had just dropped him off at work?

I called the steel mill. Yes, there was a shift change of men at that time, but they refused to give me their names.

I paced the floor for another hour or so and came up with a plan.

I went home and went to bed, sleeping little, until four o'clock in the morning. I quietly got dressed, slipped out of our house, and drove to the still closed rural service station. At exactly five o'clock, I walked out and stood in the middle of the state highway where my client told me she saw the woman drive by. Sure enough, a single car approached. I had my flashlight and clipboard, trying to look official, and I waved her down. She was startled and refused to roll her window down. I saw she had her hair in rollers and only wore a robe. I flashed my bar card to her, and she rolled down her window.

"I am investigating the shooting that took place the other morning at that gas station; I understand you saw the whole thing?" I bluffed.

"How did you know I saw it?"

She was even more startled and scared now that she had been identified and was involved.

"It is a long story, but tell me what you saw and heard that morning."

"I just dropped off my husband at the steel mill and was slowly driving home, and I noticed a black man screaming at a black woman over there, where that car is. He kept walking forward and hollering at her. She kept backing up until she was against the front of that car, and he lunged at her and grabbed the end of that gun she was pointing at him. And, *boom*, it hit him full in the chest. He spun around and fell. I got the hell out of here, so I did not get involved."

She was my missing witness, and I was blessed. I got the woman's name, address, and phone number and told her she might have to testify later in the week as to what she witnessed. She was okay with that, because she was a Christian woman and had thought about the situation since then. She was convinced the young woman just wanted the man to leave her alone and he grabbed the barrel of the gun and it exploded.

"I don't think that girl meant him any harm. At least that's what it looked like to me."

I thanked her very much for her truthfulness and public conscience and told her I would be contacting her.

Three days later, an examining trial was heard in the case before a frustrated and unprepared Oral Smith, District Attorney. He was very upset with a young lawyer, still wet behind the ears, who was forcing him and his office to prove a prima-facie murder case committed by my client.

The district attorney could only prove a man was shot with his own shotgun and that no one witnessed the shooting. I called my client to the stand, and she testified clearly to the same story she had told me.

Then I called my surprise witness, the lady I had located who saw the shooting. She testified to what she saw, and her story indicated my client was telling the truth and was simply trying to get away from the deceased at the time he grabbed the shotgun and it *exploded* into his chest.

When the witnesses finished, I made a motion for the judge to dismiss all charges against my client, because there was no evidence of a murder and that it was either an accident or self-defense by a woman in fear of her life.

The judge did his duty. He banged his gravel loudly and proclaimed, "Case dismissed; defendant ordered released," and adjourned court.

The district attorney gave me a look that could kill and walked out of the courtroom. I had made my first enemy of a district attorney. He was not the last.

My client was surprised and tearful. I took her to the jail to retrieve her personal property. She gave me a hug and her friendship ring as payment in full. Then she returned home to her baby.

I always felt I had been handsomely paid for my services in this case, because I was finally ready to defend myself on the two still pending murder cases.

The timing on all these events was quite interesting, because several weeks later, I received a phone call from Hugo, Oklahoma, to appear the following Monday morning, ready to go to trial on my criminal cases. I had mixed feelings about that call. On one hand, I just wanted to get it all over with, and on the other hand, I just wanted it all to go away so I could live a normal life.

Needless to say, my poor wife turned white as a sheet when I announced to her our need to get ready to travel back to Oklahoma for a third trial.

"I thought that mess was over with? How do they expect you to ever have a life? You are already serving a life term!" she sadly remarked.

It had been over ten years since June 19, 1963, and there was still no final determination.

———

CHAPTER 32
Final Hurdle

• • •

I DECIDED THERE WAS NO reason to pull my daughter out of school that Monday morning and alarm her. She knew nothing about my history in Hugo, Oklahoma, and my wife and I thought that it was best that she not know. How do you explain an event like that to a seven-year old child; or that her daddy might not come home ever again?

I knew from previous trials that Mondays and Tuesdays were always needed to select an *impartial* jury and that my family would not be needed for several days.

I was up and out the door at four o'clock in the morning and driving north toward the Red River Valley. It was a three-hour drive, and the old Choctaw County courthouse looked the same as ever. When I arrived, I parked and walked up those long steps one more time to the district courtroom. There were no waiting throng of jurors this time; I supposed they were coming in later in the day, after docket call.

The courtroom was fairly quiet, not what I expected. A few court personnel shuffled papers and assembled files for the morning criminal docket cases. Many new faces were apparent. In particular, there was a new district judge, recently appointed by the governor, and a newly elected county attorney, whom I had never met.

Most people thought I was just another out-of-town lawyer waiting for his client's cases to be called to trial.

Butterflies fluttered mercilessly in my stomach, and my heart pounded.

Now I really knew how criminal defendants felt when they had to appear in criminal court on their pending case. I sat at the defense counsel's table and waited for court to convene.

Everyone jumped to their feet as the district judge self-consciously took his seat behind the bench.

The court clerk handed the judge his docket sheet for the morning, and the judge loudly called the two cases pending against me. The judge looked over at me and then at the county attorney and demanded, "Where is the defendant?"

I stood quickly, and the judge stared at me.

"I am the defendant, Your Honor," I said and looked him square in the eyes, to let him know I was not a scared eighteen year-old anymore, just a scared twenty-eight year old lawyer.

The judge looked over at the county attorney, who was also now standing. "How does the state announce on these two cases, Mr. Prosecutor?"

"State is ready, Your Honor. We do have one motion to present before we go forward," he said.

"What might that be?" The judge seemed impatient with any possible delay in the proceedings.

"The state moves to dismiss both cases, Your Honor."

"What?" The judge's surprise was complete. "Dismiss two murder cases? Is that what you are requesting this court to do?" The judge's voice rose as he spoke.

"Yes, Your Honor." The county attorney sat down.

The courtroom was suddenly very quiet, as if no one quite knew what to expect next.

"The court will be adjourned for fifteen minutes. I need to check these files and the law," the judge announced. He rose and walked out the door behind the bench, into his office, and shut the door.

Several of the lawyers seated in the courtroom mumbled loud enough for everyone to hear, "The court has no option but to dismiss if the county attorney requests dismissal. It is clearly mandatory. What's he stalling for?"

The county attorney walked over and introduced himself to me.

"Bobby, it is all over. You are a free man. I am sorry it took so long."

I was not sure what to say in reply to him. I was not aware he planned to make such a motion. I had been prepared for another grueling battle, but this time, I planned to tell my story for the first time. I was a little disappointed but unsure what to do at this point. After all, this would end the matter forever.

After twenty minutes, the judge returned with a sour look on his face and briskly reconvened court.

"It would appear I have no option but to dismiss both cases, and they are therefore dismissed."

The judge never looked at me or said another word to me. He immediately called the next case on his docket as if he had just dismissed two parking tickets that were keeping him from more important matters. I took my leave.

I was sorry that the passage of time did not allow my four saviors—Mr. Hal Welch, my lawyer; Mr. Ray Kelly, my high school teacher; Mr. Rob Ford, my former employer; and Mr. Ben Dean, my church's deacon—to be there and shake my hand as I walked out of that courthouse a free man, thanks to them. Without their efforts on my behalf, I can only assume I would have spent the last ten years rotting in that county jail. All four of these gallant gentlemen had passed away over the intervening eight years.

Like many important events in a person's life, my last court appearance turned out somewhat anti-climatic. I experienced a real letdown by not having a jury fully vindicate me after hearing my story.

It was like when the system could not bury me, it would settle for a dark cloud left over my head forever.

I walked out of the courthouse after shaking a few well-wishers' hands and opened my car door and looked around one more time. I knew it would be many years before I would ever see this place again, if ever.

I called my wife and told her the news; she almost fainted and was crying when I hung up the phone.

I started the drive back to my home, wondering what was in my future.

I had decided, after watching the Vietnam disaster unfold over the last ten years that my previous plans for a military career would have probably resulted in my blood soaking into some worthless rice patty in Asia. I had worked in a re-training program at Safeway to help returning shell-shocked Vietnam veterans, and I witnessed firsthand the ruined lives our government's great mistake had produced.

I also knew that I would always be a controversial figure in the legal community because I would not be the type of criminal defense lawyer content to just get with the program and help feed my clients into the hungry jaws of our legal system. Many a judge and prosecutor would come to hate my guts, which was fine with me. I could always look myself in the mirror each morning without shame. At least my clients appreciated my efforts, and their freedom.

I never had the opportunity to tell my version of what happened in those early morning hours of June 19, 1963. I was widely misquoted, and often just plain slandered, in the press, and I guess that is why I wrote this book—so the public could truly know what occurred during that ordeal.

I have always believed, and still do, that the three investigative agents, Sheriff Thornton, County Attorney Jenner, and newspaper publisher Jack Stamper knew from the very beginning of this investigation that my mother was probably insane that fateful morning. When she came home that day, she had hell to pay on her mind, and my sister and I were innocent victims of her rage.

But it made better press for said actors to focus a murder investigation on me. It was political gold for Jenner and

Thorton, and great story writing and paper selling for Stamper. It was also a good way to avoid paying a fire insurance claim for Agent Carmichael's employers.

The truth is an absolute defense to a libel and slander claim, so I have no fear in making any of these allegations.

Fire and arson experts, such as Carmichael and Stringer, always knew that no one could pour gallons of gasoline around the inside of a closed house and stand *within* that house and light a match. No person could have survived that blast or the inferno that would follow.

Therefore, they always knew I never poured gasoline in that house and lit a match. They examined the wooden screen window that was blown fifteen feet from that house, the only surviving window screen, and saw the outline of my body on the screen and the blood from the glass cuts on my hands and body. My jeans were bloody, but no one bothered to test the blood to see if it was mine or someone else's. Their only statements to the public were that I had washed and changed clothes, before the fire. They knew better, but again, it just did not fit their story.

The .22 rifle with the broken stock was never hidden. It was thrown in a roadside ditch, not buried in the deep woods as they stated to the press. They found no bullet in my mother's body, so they had no way to match a bullet with any of the two .22 caliber rifles that were in that house that morning. No one bothered to look for fingerprints on the rifle that was recovered or to test its broken stock for signs of human tissue.

There was never any evidence that I had harmed my sister or had any reason to wish her harm.

So what did happen that morning?

I did not know myself for almost ten years, and then that odor of gasoline mixing with blood brought my memory of those events back to me in a terrible flood.

I had been in a deep sleep that morning, when suddenly I was startled by my mother shaking me violently and shouting, "Get up!"

"I don't have any pants on," I said.

"Get up now!" The barrel of my .22 caliber Mossberg fully loaded semi-automatic was pointed at me.

I slid my feet out from under the bed covers, turned my back on my mother, and pulled up my jeans, when she screamed again.

"Don't turn your back on me, you sorry bastard. Think you can leave me for some worthless bitch like your father did? I'll show you."

I turned around to face the rifle barrel and the crazed look of a woman out of her mind. She was going to shoot me. I had no doubt. I reached up and pulled the ceiling light string, and the only light source in my room was gone. The room was immediately totally black.

I fell to the floor and crawled on my hands and knees behind my steel frame bed, trying to hide and looking for cover.

Blam Blam Blam Blam Blam Blam. She started shooting, six times. Muzzle flashes and bullets flew all across my room. Bullets and empty shells struck the walls, the floor, and the steel bed frame of my bed and ricocheted all around. I heard glass breaking and things falling from the walls. A shadow moved through the open door of our adjoining bedrooms, and Mother thought it was me. She was startled, and her shadow swung that Mossberg rifle by its barrel like a baseball bat. There was a sickening thud and moan and another loud bang and moan as a body crashed into the steel headboard of my bed frame and fell to the floor.

It was completely quiet for a moment, except for someone's heavy breathing and a sickening rattling sound coming from my bedroom floor.

I had always kept my small single-shot .22 caliber rifle under my bed, fully loaded for the many times I had to grab it in the middle of the night when Butch would corner a hungry possum or skunk in our henhouse. I would quickly dispatch the chicken thief and return to bed while still half asleep. I usually left Butch to clean up the mess.

I looked over the top of my bed and could see Mother's shadow under that single ceiling light bulb. She held the rifle in one hand and was trying to find that string with the other hand as she turned in slow circles while trying to turn on that light bulb.

I knew I was a dead man if she managed to turn on that light. There was no question in my mind now that she had gone completely crazy and would kill me and anyone else who got in her way.

I only had one chance to survive this encounter, and I took it. I raised and pointed the short rifle toward where her head should be, and I fired. She collapsed near my bed without a sound.

I pulled myself up with one hand on my bed, reached for that still swinging light string, and pulled it. I was greeted by the most horrible sight a boy could possibly encounter.

Lying in a bloody heap on the floor was my mother, on top of my sister. Both were bleeding profusely from head wounds. Both were still breathing heavily and slowly.

One of my mother's eyes was gone; just a bloody eye socket remained. Sister's long brown hair was heavily matted in blood. Blood was everywhere. Mother still had her work clothes on. Sister was in her pajamas, now soaked in blood.

My adrenaline was pumping, and my heart was racing. I seemed to have super human strength. My mother weighed as much as me. I lifted my mother off my sister's body, quickly carried her to the adjoining bedroom, laid her down, and cleared her airway. She was struggling for breath. I ran back into my bedroom and my feet went out from under me, and I fell into a mixture of gasoline and blood.

The bedroom floor was a mass of liquid, very slippery, and a mixture of yellow and red. That is when that strange odor hit me, like nothing I ever smelled before, utterly sickening, pungent, and nauseating.

I picked up my sister's totally limp body out of the fluid mess and started to put her body on my bed. But the gasoline fumes in the room got very bad, so I carried her into her bedroom and closed the door to try to keep the fumes out. Sister was not responding and was no longer bleeding. She must have stumbled into my bedroom trying to find out what was causing all the noise. She was the shadow at which Mother swung the rifle.

I tripped over the broken Mossberg .22 caliber rifle Mother had used, which I had kicked around on the floor when I had carried her into the bedroom. I picked it up and ran into the living room to use our one phone to call for an ambulance. When I pulled on the light switch in the living room, there was a bright flash and explosion of gasoline fumes, and I was propelled through the living room window into the wet field of grass. My head slammed into a fence post when I hit the ground, and everything was a blur after that.

By the time I was released from the hospital, I could not remember a thing that happened other than Mother waking me and pointing a rifle in my face and an odor I could not ascertain.

The rest is history.

I found the broken rifle in that field and Mother's '59 Ford full of my clothes when I returned from the hospital. I have no idea how the rifle or the clothes came to be where I found them that morning.

Obviously, the bottles of gasoline stored in my bedroom had been broken, and the fumes reached ignition point and probably exploded when I turned on the living room light bulb.

It was a horrible event, caused by a woman gone insane and out of control. None of the events made any sense, so the various actors twisted around the facts until it made sense, at least to them. I am sure there is a special place in hell for folks of that mindset.

My lovely, sweet sister Judy, was the only true innocent. She deserved a better life, and may she rest in peace.

THE END

EPILOGUE

When I decided to write this book, I again became curious about my mother's heritage. I enlisted my private investigation firm to find the answers to the mystery of my mother's history.

The results of that investigation startled me.

Lavonne Wilson was not my mother's name. She had changed her identity sometime in her past. Her real name was Nellie Winkler. She was born in Wagner, Oklahoma, in either 1910 or 1911; there was no birth certificate.

Mother's parents were George and Callie Winkler. Mother had two older sisters, Arie and Goldie Winkler, from that marriage.

Callie Winkler abandoned her husband, George, a few months after my mother's birth, and ran away with their servant, Alec (J.A.) Cross and her three daughters. They settled in Choctaw County, Oklahoma, near Hugo, Oklahoma, sometime before 1920. Callie then gave birth to four more children with her new husband, three boys and one girl. The girl died later under mysterious circumstances, from severe burns.

Callie then abandoned all six of her surviving children, which included my mother, leaving them with Alec Cross to raise, and ran off to California with a traveling salesman. She died in California in 1957 after numerous other men passed through her life.

Several of Callie's surviving relatives described her as having extreme bouts of depression and wild schizophrenic outbursts during her lifetime. She feared no man.

My mother's sister, Arie, died in Phoenix, Arizona, in 1938. Mother's other sister, Goldie, and her supposed father, George Winkler, died in Oklahoma in 1970.

One of my mother's half-brothers still lives in Oklahoma and told me my mother ran away from home when she was about sixteen years old and was never heard from again by any family members. No one knew of her change of name or why she fled.

I have spoken directly with several other of my mother's surviving family members who knew Callie Winkler well, and when I describe my mother's actions and behavior toward me, they all say, "She sounds just like *her mother*."

The last known family photograph of Mother's family, which was taken within days of her mother running off with their servant, reveals my mother was a dark-haired baby with Indian facial features when compared to her two older, very blond sisters. Maybe she really did have a Cherokee chief father, about whom she always bragged.

My mother had lived out her life only a few miles from her family and relatives but never made any effort to contact them. They probably shopped in the Hugo, Oklahoma grocery store I worked in, and we were ships passing in the night.

I located her 1937 Social Security application, and she was living under the name of Lavonne Wilson at that time. No marriages, divorces, etc. could be located on her.

So why did she change her name and then return to her home county and avoid her relatives? Your guess is as good as mine.

So whom was Mother running and hiding from? I never knew. I suspect, only her demons.

I practiced rough-and-tumble criminal and civil trial law for many years until I stepped on so many prosecutors and judges' toes I decided to resign and sold my law practice and became a college law professor and writer.

Since then, besides teaching and writing, I have been developing college law and paralegal courses. I also organized and own one of the top private investigation firms in the United States, Arizona Undercover Private Investigations, Inc.

True tales of some of my more controversial civil and criminal trials are the subject of my next book, *Bobby's Trials, Part II*, which will be released in the fall of 2010.

So stay tuned to www.bobbystrials.com for further announcements.

———